THE LIBERAL DILEMMA

The Liberal Dilemma

ALAN WATKINS

MACGIBBON & KEE

First published 1966 by MacGibbon & Kee, Ltd.

Printed in Great Britain by
Clarke, Doble & Brendon, Ltd.
Cattedown, Plymouth

CONTENTS

PREFACE

THIS BOOK is not intended as a detailed history of the post-war Liberal Party. Nor is it concerned with the day-to-day activities of the Liberals in Parliament. Nor, again, is it a work of sociology or of psephology—though from time to time I give skeletal election figures. It deals not with political tactics but with political strategy. It attempts to answer the question: where, since the war, has the Liberal Party stood in relation to the main parties? It is primarily a study of the party in its external relations.

Dr J. S. Rasmussen's book *The Liberal Party* appeared when I was completing my writing. His book and mine are, I would hope, complementary rather than conflicting.

I did not ask the Liberal Party for any official help in the gathering of material for the book. The information I mainly required was readily available from published sources and from sources normally open to me in my work as a political correspondent. And in any case I thought it better that in a book of this kind there should be no suspicion of party approval—though I am confident that, if I had asked, facilities would have been granted unconditionally. However, I should like to thank Mr Pratap Chitnis who, with his usual efficiency, cleared up various points of detail.

Other assistance was given by Mr Mark Bonham Carter, Mr Edward Martell and the late Lady Megan Lloyd George. The staffs of the libraries of the *Daily Express*, *The Times* and the London School of Economics and Political Science were unfailingly helpful. Mrs Henrietta Gledhill, Mrs Pauline Elliot, Mrs Diana Kirk and Miss Cecilia Hurst typed successive chunks of the MS, often in difficult circumstances. To all of these I am grateful.

Above all, I would thank Mr R. G. Davis-Poynter of MacGibbon & Kee for his encouragement and for his patience in dealing with a dilatory author.

Chertsey A.W.
16 May 1966

CHAPTER I

MR GRIMOND: A NEW LIBERAL

'Time which antiquates antiquities, and hath an art to make dust of all things, hath yet spared these minor monuments'.

SIR THOMAS BROWNE: *Urn Burial.*

I

THE stability of the British political system has frequently been celebrated as the envy of the foreigner and the wonder of the wise. What has been remarked perhaps less frequently is the unpredictability of our politics as they operate from day to day. The reputations of Ministers rise and fall; policies go in and out of fashion; questions that are disputed ferociously one year are hardly discussed the next. For instance, how many Conservative politicians would now rate Mr Harold Macmillan as one of the greatest peace-time Prime Ministers? Under two years ago his claims in this direction were being advanced with the greatest conviction. Whoever now hears of the non-nuclear club? Not so far back Labour defence pundits were earnestly pressing its merits. Or, again, what became of the argument about the 'alternative' to British membership of the Common Market? Everyone now admits that there was never any real question of an alternative—except for Britain to stay out and work harder.

Occasionally these curious shifts and turns can be explained rationally: more often than not, they cannot. More often than not, also, it does not very much matter whether they can be so explained or not. The two great parties move confidently on, supported by great interests in the State. Sometimes the major parties may hesitate a little, sometimes they may appear to have fundamental doubts as to the wisdom of their policies or the ability of their leaders or even their chances of survival. But such moments are rare. One that comes readily to mind is the Labour Party's experience in 1959-61. Another is the Conservative Party's period of guilt and frustration after Suez. For most of the time, however, the leaders and the members of the two main parties have a good idea of where they are going, and why.

The Liberal Party since 1945 has only rarely managed to show or feel such self-confidence. It has been much more at the mercy of political events. Second place in a by-election, and the revival is well under way. Third place in another by-election a few months later, and the revival is thought to have suffered a set-back. A win at Torrington or at Orpington, however, and the revival is believed to be an established fact which will change the face of British politics. Yet precisely what is it that is being revived? Are modern Liberals the descendants of Gladstone, or of Asquith, or of Lloyd George? Or are they descendants of none of these? Is the Liberal Party to be the party of free enterprise? Or is it to favour regulation of the economy by the State? And, if so, how much regulation is there to be? Is the Liberal Party to be anti-Conservative, or anti-Socialist, or a party of the centre? Different answers to these questions have been given by different post-war Liberals. There has sometimes been doubt, sometimes, even, terrible wrestling of the spirit, among the members of the party. But there has not been the slightest doubt in the mind of Mr Jo Grimond. Mr Grimond has succeeded to a remarkable extent in moulding the modern Liberal Party in accordance with his own beliefs and personality; and to these we must now turn.

II

Jo Grimond—he has always preferred the abbreviation, though it was not widely adopted by the Press until after his election as leader—was born in St Andrews, Fifeshire, on 29 July 1913. His father was a successful jute merchant. He was educated at Eton and at Balliol College, Oxford, where he was Brackenbury Scholar and obtained first-class honours in Philosophy, Politics and Economics. In 1938 he married Laura, the daughter of Lady Violet Bonham Carter. Following war service in the Army he worked for UNRRA, became Secretary of the National Trust for Scotland, and was in 1950 elected Liberal M.P. for Orkney and Shetland. Six years later Mr Grimond succeeded Clement Davies as leader of the party.

At first sight Mr Grimond is a modest man. He walks quickly through the corridors of Westminster, his head down, his pockets stuffed full of papers. It is a self-effacing, almost a wall-brushing walk. Unlike many other M.P.s who hold far less impressive positions in their parties, he shows no desire to draw attention to himself. Yet, with his crisp grey hair, his unusual combination of scholarly stoop and athletic stride, his restrained tweeds, Mr Grimond can hardly escape being noticed. Despite his best endeavours to be anonymous, he cannot quite manage it. His conversation fits harmoniously with this appearance. It is light, unpompous, incisive. But, above all, Mr Grimond's talk is objective and sometimes almost self-mocking. And it is this quality which distinguishes it from that of other leading politicians. For most Members who have attained prominent positions in their own parties are unpompous and incisive when they are not making public speeches. They joke about their party, about their colleagues, sometimes even about themselves. But they never—or very, very rarely—express any basic doubt about the value or importance of the activity in which they are engaged. Mr Grimond is different. And it is this scepticism about politics, as they operate in practice, which makes him such an interesting figure.

Yet is this genuine modesty on Mr Grimond's part? Could it be, on the contrary, an example of Whig arrogance? Certainly he contrives to preserve something of the eighteenth century's detachment. Indeed there are in Mr Grimond echoes of Lord Melbourne. When, for example, Mr Grimond attacked the honours system six years ago, was he delivering a radical onslaught upon class and privilege? Or was he expressing a well-bred contempt for awards which had 'no damned merit' about them? There is room for argument. 'He had', it was written of Melbourne, 'learnt to play the political game with practised skill; but like a grown-up person playing hide-and-seek with children, he never entered completely into the spirit of the thing. His thought moved from a different centre and on different lines. And he was much too candid not to show it.'[1] Very much the same words could appropriately be applied today to Mr Grimond—though there must remain some doubt as to the degree of skill he exhibits in playing the political game.

[1] D. Cecil, *Lord M.*, Grey Arrow edn. (1962), p. 39.

III

It is obvious that there are dangers in Mr Grimond's approach to politics. A contempt for their day-to-day workings can lead to a contempt for political democracy. Dissatisfaction with the existing forms of parliamentary government, which Mr Grimond has frequently expressed, can lead to dissatisfaction with parliamentary government itself. 'In a sense . . .', wrote Mr Peregrine Worsthorne, 'the very quality of simple, boyish straightforwardness with which Mr Grimond answers questions is the most sinister thing about him. For although he is actually in the business of seduction he preserves the manner of the innocent flirt. An occasional blush, an evasion or two, a hint of duplicity, would surely be much more reassuring, since then we would know that at least he respected the inevitable limitations of democratic politics. Beware of magicians, the more so when they are so enchantingly the victim of their own spells.'[2]

It is difficult to imagine Mr Grimond, who is so obviously honest, so obviously kindly, so obviously a democrat, leading a revolutionary *putsch*. Nevertheless, the arguments which he constantly advances inevitably tend towards a weakening of confidence in British parliamentary government. And Mr Grimond cannot really be blamed for this: it arises naturally from the situation in which the Liberal Party finds itself. A third party in an essentially two-party system is bound to try to cast doubts on the system itself. At one time the Liberals confined themselves to demands for proportional representation, or other alterations in electoral law and organization. Mr Grimond, however, changed all this. He took the view that potential Liberal voters would be bored and irritated by cries of 'It's not fair'. Instead he concentrated on more fundamental and far-reaching criticisms of our politics.

Was Mr Grimond aware of the perils? 'The most dangerous attacks on freedom in a democracy', he has written, 'come from those who are irritated by the democratic process.'[3] Yet irritation with the democratic process, as it actually operates, is what Mr Grimond exhibits. Let us take, for example, his criticisms of Parlia-

[2] *Sunday Telegraph*, 20 May 1962.
[3] J. Grimond, *The Liberal Challenge* (1963), p. 28.

ment. 'A striking feature of House of Commons politics today', he writes, 'is that many of the most politically able Members seldom attend, hardly ever ask questions and speak infrequently. The reason is . . . that so much of our procedure is time-wasting and ill-directed, and shows little result.'[4] Again, he criticises the House of Commons on the grounds that 'there are important questions which neither the Government nor the leaders of the official Opposition may want to debate in public at all. For several years this was true of defence owing to disagreements within the Labour Party and it is still true of strikes. But when a debate on some large topic of supposed political interest does take place, what is it supposed to do? Parliament has two debating chambers: but they are not for the airing of views to no purpose. They are for bringing debate to bear on Ministers.'

Clearly Mr Grimond's intentions are of the best. He can argue with complete conviction that he is concerned not to belittle the democratic process but to make it more fully democratic. However, the actual processes of government in a country such as Britain are not means towards an abstract end called 'democracy'. They constitute the end itself. And it is perhaps significant that, while Mr Grimond was lamenting the inadequacies of parliamentary procedure, Mr Harold Wilson was making use of that procedure both on the floor of the House and, for a time, as Chairman of the Public Accounts Committee. Indeed, whatever effect Mr Grimond's lack of enthusiasm for Parliament may have had on people generally, there can be little dispute about its effect on his own party.

IV

For the Liberals at Westminster have not glittered under Mr Grimond. The air of dash and bravura which they have possessed in the country has been left behind in New Palace Yard. It is difficult to recall any issue fought out on the floor of the Commons which the Liberals have made peculiarly their own. It is difficult to recall any parliamentary campaign which they have initiated, still less brought to a successful conclusion.

What can account for this failure? Certainly a parliamentary force of between five and seven presents difficulties. For instance, Mr Donald Wade, M.P., explained, in answer to criticisms of

[4] ibid. p. 105.

Liberal division records, that 'there is, of course, continuous pressure on Liberal M.P.s to fulfil duties in the country as well as carry out their many obligations at Westminster'.[5] But pressure of duties outside Westminster, though naturally greater in a party with a small parliamentary representation, is hardly an adequate explanation for this lack of impact. After all, did not Lord Randolph Churchill and his small band of rebels seriously put out the Conservative leadership of their day? Did not the Irish party bring Parliament to a standstill with their intransigence? Mr Arthur Holt, M.P., was asked at a press conference about the contrast between the old Irish party and the new Liberal. He replied, somewhat lamely one feels, that 'the Irish party had only one purpose, whereas we have the whole field of politics'.[6]

Yet, outside Westminster Mr Grimond has shown a certain tactical sense in choosing a limited number of issues on which to make major pronouncements of policy. Once inside the House, however, and this tactical sense deserts him. On the floor of the Commons, at least, Mr Grimond is reluctant to kick up a fuss. Harrying the Government does not come naturally to him. When one thinks of the impression made by some other M.P.s, this reluctance on Mr Grimond's part seems a pity. Mr Sydney Silverman on capital punishment, Sir Gerald Nabarro on purchase tax, Mr George Wigg on army manpower (and, of course, on the Profumo affair): all have shown what can be done by a determined Member. And how much more could be done by seven determined Members, acting in concert?

Mr Grimond might reply that the kind of success achieved by Mr Silverman or Sir Gerald or Mr Wigg does not particularly interest him. 'The sort of mistakes which must be exploited,' he has written sorrowfully, 'are those which get good publicity in the popular Press or which adversely affect certain interests. These are by no means always the most serious errors of government, if indeed they are errors at all. The need for publicity corrupts as much or more than power. The temptation to win by taking up a series of grievances, even if some of them are unjustified, is a hazard of politics.'[7] It is a temptation to which Mr Grimond has rarely if ever fallen victim.

[5] Letter in *Sunday Telegraph*, 10 December 1961.
[6] *Daily Express*, 6 September 1962.
[7] J. Grimond, *The Liberal Challenge* (1963), p. 42.

Further, Mr Grimond might ask, what evidence is there that even the most weighty parliamentary victories, even those which attract no vulgar publicity, gain any extra votes in the country? There is, perhaps, rather more evidence than is generally allowed—though it is not of the kind that can be measured or tabulated. What we are concerned with here is not the effect of a single parliamentary triumph. Nor is it even the cumulative effect of a succession of victories in parliament. It is, rather, the way in which a general parliamentary reputation becomes known in the country as a whole. It is the curious process of transpiration whereby the judgments made in the lobbies and corridors and bars of the Palace of Westminster communicate themselves to the people. That such a process does indeed take place is in the last resort a matter for personal observation. But there are also several illustrations from which the process can be inferred.

Hugh Gaitskell first became accepted as a national figure when, towards the end of his life, he acquired a mastery over the House of Commons greater even than that of Mr. Harold Macmillan. (And, of course, at about this time, when Mr Macmillan's command over the House became less easy, his public reputation diminished). Again, Mr Wilson's remarkably quick acceptance as a major politician may owe as much to his debating skill as to his 'projection'. Television, after all, is hardly the whole of politics. It has often been said that the British people do not believe everything they read in the newspapers. It is equally true, though said less often, that they do not believe everything they see on television. If they did, Mr Grimond might be Prime Minister.

Nor is it only the parliamentary reputations of individuals that become widely recognized. The same process can be observed working where whole parties are concerned. The revival of the Conservative Party after the 1945 debacle was due not only to the well-known efforts of Mr R. A. Butler but also to the parliamentary performance put up by men like Oliver Stanley.[8] And the decline of the Labour Party in parliament, towards the end of its first post-war period of government, undoubtedly had its effect on the electorate.

These considerations are given no weight by Mr Grimond. And, as we have seen from his writings, this omission is not due to idleness on his part. It is not, again, that he has inadequate talent

[8] cf. John Freeman in the *New Statesman*, 14 November 1959.

or resources at his disposal. Rather it arises from a theoretical doubt as to the results which are likely to be gained from day-to-day parliamentary activity.

V

What makes the Liberal parliamentary failure more surprising is the wealth of ideas which Mr Grimond has had at his disposal. He has, moreover, tried to make these ideas part of a political philosophy. In his sadly underestimated[9] book *The Liberal Challenge* an attitude towards the problems of society, the individual and the State does emerge. 'For me', writes Mr Grimond, 'Liberalism is not about *laissez-faire* or Free Trade or indeed any economic doctrine. It is about the broader questions of humanity and society or, if about economics, then about the wider sort of political economy on which Adam Smith wrote. It is about man and his society and the type of government he wants to regulate that society. It has been said that Socialism is about Equality. If you ask for an equivalent shorthand description of Liberalism I should say that it is about Freedom and Participation.'[10] Clearly, then, Mr Grimond is no doctrinaire Liberal. Indeed he believes that the heaviest handicap from which his party has suffered is its association with 'economic doctrines which few Liberals ever held in their extreme form'. The humanitarian basis of Liberalism, Mr Grimond thinks, has been forgotten too long.[11]

But it is doubtful whether such Liberal humanitarians as Gladstone and Morley would have been able to concur with Mr Grimond's views on government and society. Even J. S. Mill, who at the end of his life was a near-Socialist, would have been a little taken aback by some of Mr Grimond's thoughts. In a sentence which might have come straight out of a *Tribune* pamphlet, he says that 'it is because of the fact that the vast percentage of the wealth of the country is owned by a tiny fraction of the population that the capitalist system as at present organized is fundamentally unstable'.[12] Mr Grimond's remedy for this state of affairs is not nationalization or increased taxation but co-partnership in industry. Co-partnership, of course, is one of those hallowed phrases of modern Liberalism—proportional representation and

[9] Except by Professor Bernard Crick in the *Observer*, 27 October 1963.
[10] J. Grimond, *The Liberal Challenge* (1963), p. 23.
[11] ibid. p. 33. [12] ibid. p. 157.

the taxation of site values are two others—which are used by most party members as incantations rather than as meaningful political terms. But Mr Grimond is different. For him, co-partnership is more than a phrase. It is also more than an accountant's device for giving workers a share of company profits. He believes that workers should participate in the control of their companies. He is very close to being an old-fashioned Syndicalist. 'If,' he writes, 'there had been no First World War, if there had been a synthesis of Liberals and Labour in 1929, if Guild Socialism or Syndicalism had not been rejected, we might have had a continuation of the main flood of progressive thought. But we did not. Belief in the State and State Socialism dominated politics between the wars. This was to be the main road forward for the Left.'[13]

Nor is it only that Mr Grimond professes a most un-Liberal faith in the virtues of workers' control. At a more fundamental level he has great confidence in the efficacy of Government action. He writes that 'human beings, huddling together in terror of being left alone, baffled by the prison of their own sensations, long for some support, for some assurance that they are of importance, that life has "meaning". Before they face the ultimate loneliness of death they look for some assurance that their endeavours on earth have some immortality. Society and the State as its servant must help to meet this yearning.'[14] There is no doubt that this is a passage with a certain nobility about it. There is equally no doubt that it presents a pretty tall order to any government. Whether the State should try to fill the need which Mr Grimond outlines is arguable: but what is surely not arguable is that a traditional Liberal would regard any such attempt with horror.

It may be objected, of course, that the views of political parties and their leaders are changing all the time. The Conservative Party under Sir Alec Douglas-Home is recognizably a different animal from the Conservative Party under Stanley Baldwin. The last three leaders of the Labour Party have possessed markedly divergent views about the basis of Socialism: Lord Attlee, a Toynbee Hall philanthropist; Gaitskell, a doctrinaire egalitarian; Mr Wilson, with his greater emphasis on opportunity. Surely the Liberal Party ought to be allowed a similar latitude; perhaps, even,

[13] ibid. p. 299. And see J. Grimond, 'Why the Barons Went'. *Time and Tide*, 15 February 1962.
[14] ibid. p. 205.

a greater one? Is it not in the nature of Liberalism to favour changed solutions in the face of changed circumstances? And, after all, Gladstone would hardly have approved many of the actions of the 1906 Liberal Government.[15] Why should not Mr Grimond be allowed to give modern Liberalism whatever content he chooses?

One answer is that a party based on no clearly defined material interest can find a unifying force in tradition. Or, to put the same point in a slightly different way, the personal ascendancy of Mr. Grimond in the Liberal Party has led to the most curious interpretations of Liberalism by some of his followers, who have little else but Mr Grimond to guide them. Time and again in the past few years declarations of policy have been issued which have little internal consistency, hardly any correlation with one another and no connection with any body of Liberal principles. For example, a committee of thirteen Liberals under the chairmanship of Mr Eric Lubbock, M.P., recommended that old people who lived in houses too big for them should be encouraged to move to other accommodation even if they were owner-occupiers. Simultaneously the committee (which was set up by the party executive in 1961) wanted people to be encouraged to own their homes. It called for the immediate abolition of Schedule A taxation and of stamp duty on mortgages.[16]

It may seem unkind to saddle Mr Grimond with responsibility for pronouncements of this kind. Yet in one sense he is indeed responsible. Though he has worked out a new version of Liberalism to his own satisfaction, his less theoretically minded supporters have been left stranded. They are preoccupied with what will appear to be modern, brisk and efficient. There is to be more freedom for back-bench M.P.s: but parliamentary procedure is to be speeded up. Local government will be re-invigorated: but at the same time the powers of the central government to plan regionally will be increased. There is a reluctance to admit that priorities have to be established, prices to be paid.

All this is not to derogate from Mr Grimond's achievement in giving his party a fairly clear policy on some of the major questions of the past few years: on the independent deterrent, on

[15] cf. A. V. Dicey's criticisms in his Introduction to the 2nd edn. (1919) of *Law and Public Opinion in England.*

[16] *Sunday Times*, 16 September 1962.

British entry into the Common Market, above all on the role of the Liberals themselves in British politics. On all these matters the Leader has spoken with a firm and clear voice; and, by and large, his followers inside the party have been in full agreement with him. Miss Manuela Sykes may have been less than fully committed to going into Europe; Lord Moynihan may have jibbed at the anti-Conservative trends in the party; Colonel Patrick Lort-Phillips may have indulged his rebellious feelings: but, nevertheless, the disaffected and the disloyal, the Adullamites and the backsliders have on major issues been in a minority. In particular Mr Grimond's decision to replace Labour with a radical Liberal party struck sympathetic chords with the younger members. A typical expression of this decision is to be found in a speech he delivered in June 1962. The party's future role, said Mr Grimond, would be to share the Left with Labour. He rejected any idea that it should become a centre party; that had no place in our present constitution. The place of the Liberal Party was on the progressive and the Left side of politics. Mr Grimond forecast a radical change in the structure of politics, and eventually 200 Liberal M.P.s. There would also be a Labour Party which really believed in Socialism, nationalization and State control directly exercised on industry. And on the other side would be the Tories, who do not have a positive view of government'.[17]

VI

Yet to what extent was this view of the Liberals' role approved, or even appreciated, by the people who actually voted Liberal? Did these voters, moreover, know of the party's clear policy on, say, the deterrent and the Common Market? There is a certain amount of evidence, which will be examined in greater detail later,[18] of a dissociation between, on the one hand, the Liberal leadership and active workers and, on the other, the Liberal voters. For instance, in Dr Mark Abrams's post-Orpington survey, there is the fact that 36 per cent of the voters agreed with the proposition that 'the Liberal Party has not really got a clear-cut policy'.[19] And, as Mr Blondel observed, 'one of the difficulties of the Liberal party seems

[17] Report in *Daily Express*, 15 June 1962.
[18] See below, pp. 118ff.
[19] M. Abrams, 'Who are the New Liberals?' *Observer*, 1 July 1962.

to be that it does not, as yet, evoke any images in the minds of the electors'.[20]

Of course, the Liberal Party is by no means alone in failing to make its policy clear to its supporters. And political writers from Bagehot onwards have pointed to the gap which exists between any party's activists and its supporters in the country. But the case of the Liberals seems to be different in kind from that of the Conservatives or the Labour Party. Labour voters, for instance, generally have a fairly good idea of the nature of the party they are voting for, and why. Some of their ideas about the party, it is true, may be a little rough and ready; their reasons for voting as they do, if given at all, may vary enormously; their real motives may vary in the same way. But, despite all this, they are talking about what is recognizably the same political organization. Hardly one Labour voter would suppose, say, that his party stood for the interests of stockbrokers against those of factory workers. The modern Liberal Party, however, has not been pinned down to anything like the same extent by its supporters. Their characteristics, and their reasons for voting Liberal, are correspondingly wider.

Why do people vote Liberal? Dr Richard Rose has suggested the following classification of the party's support:

(i) The anti-political voter, the man of good will who does not think parties ought to disagree about what is best for the nation. He votes Liberal because it looks least like a political party and because its programme is broad enough to embrace many views.

(ii) The anti-class conflict voter: a social equivalent of the anti-political voter. He resents class divisions, but believes that the way to attack them politically is by voting for the party which is not associated with any class.

(iii) The socially responsive voter, who acts with reference to conflicting social pressures, and solves them by compromise. He may be cross-pressured, for example, by his workmates to vote Labour and by his family to vote Conservative. He resolves the conflict by voting Liberal.

(iv) The half-way house voter. His motive is to express withdrawal of support from his old party without helping its major opponent. He is in evidence at by-elections particularly.[21] Clearly

[20] J. Blondel, *Voters, Parties and Leaders* (1963), p. 83.

[21] R. Rose, 'How the Party System Works' in M. Abrams and Rose, *Must Labour Lose*? (1960), pp. 95-6.

these categories are not mutually exclusive. Nor are they exhaustive. A man may vote Liberal simply because he likes Mr Grimond, or because he honestly believes that the party provides the best answer to what he conceives to be Britain's problems. He may vote Liberal because his family has always done so, or because Lloyd George knew his father. Human behaviour, in the polling-booth or elsewhere, is not susceptible of easy classification, even when reasons and motives are fully known. And in the case of voting behaviour these facts are not sufficiently established. Having said this, however, there is no reason why hypotheses should not be framed, and as far as possible, tested. Political writers should perhaps be permitted at least as much freedom as theoretical economists.

Thus Mr A. J. Allen attributes the post-1945 Liberal revival to the public's boredom, frustration and resentment with the other two parties 'which seemed to be perpetually fighting a very wordy battle over the merits of nationalization, de-nationalization and re-nationalization'. The genesis of this feeling, Mr Allen believes, was the political situation of the early 1950's 'when Buskellism ruled the day, as if, by keeping quiet about the true nature of our political and economic problems, they would simply go away'. It is not perhaps a coincidence, he writes, that the end of this period was marked by the Inverness by-election of December 1954.[22] 'It is surely significant,' Mr Allen goes on, 'that the most dedicated Liberal seat in the House today (i.e. Orkney and Shetland) is the furthest removed from Westminster, a measure of the discontent with the Central Government in the far-flung regions which manifests itself in the sporadic boosts in support for Welsh and Scottish nationalist candidates.'[23]

Though Mr Allen's industrious analysis of voting patterns has put students in his debt, the reasons he gives for the Liberal revival may be questioned. For one thing, few Liberals would now claim that the 1951-5 period was a particularly inspiring one in the party's history. On the contrary, it was characterized by poor by-election results, desertions from the ranks and growing dissatisfaction with the leadership of Clement Davies. The work of

[22] 1954: N. L. D. McLean (C.), 10,329; J. M. Bannerman (Lib.), 8,998; W. Paterson (Lab.), 5,642; C. maj., 1,331. 1951: Lord M. Douglas-Hamilton (C.), 22,497; T. A. Macnair (Lab.), 12,361; C. maj., 10,136.

[23] A. J. Allen, *The English Voter* (1964), p. 40.

the Radical Reform Group[23a] did not begin to show dividends until after Mr Grimond had taken over. The Inverness by-election result was of course a good one: but it can hardly be interpreted as nationally significant. First, Mr John Bannerman is possibly the best-known Liberal in Scotland, with the exception of Mr Grimond himself. (Indeed it is always predicted of Mr Bannerman that he is about to bring off some spectacular win at the polls; a prediction which in the event is always falsified.) Second, Inverness is, if a Liberal citadel at all, one of old-fashioned Liberalism. In fact election results from the rural areas of Scotland and Wales cannot prove very much about the success or otherwise of modern Liberalism. For this reason the defeat of the Liberal candidate at Carmarthen in 1957, coming as it did immediately before some encouraging by-election performances elsewhere, was not nationally significant; and similarly not a great deal can be deducted from Mr Grimond's established position at Orkney and Shetland.

Other commentators fix the beginning of the Liberal revival somewhat later. The movement is assumed to be a post-Suez, post-Grimond phenomenon. The causes are said to include a disgust with the 'cynicism' of Mr Macmillan's administration and an antipathy towards a 'cloth-cap' Labour Party. The whole phenomenon is linked to an increase in material prosperity and a rise in the number of white-collar jobs. Those who explain Liberalism in this way may conveniently be described as belonging to the spin-drier school; and Mr Woodrow Wyatt can be taken as one example. Addressing the Bosworth Constituency Labour Party following the Orpington result, Mr Wyatt declared that 'there is a new social group emerging. It is young. It is white collar. It is skilled. It is ambitious to advance socially and economically. It will decide the next election. It does not want the Tories but it does not want a cloth-cap Labour Party either.'[24] Mr Wyatt was, of course, a prominent supporter of Hugh Gaitskell in the Labour Party controversy over nuclear disarmament and Clause IV; and subsequently he put forward a scheme for an electoral agreement between Labour and the Liberals. He may not unfairly be described as a persuader rather than an analyser: but for an analysis we can turn to Mr Anthony Crosland.

[23a] For which see below, pp. 69ff.

[24] *Observer*, 18 March 1962.

In his commentaries that followed the 1959 election Mr Crosland was concerned principally with the Labour Party and its fortunes: inevitably the Liberal Party was peripheral to his argument. Nevertheless, what he had to say about the Liberals and their prospects is worth examining in the present context. Briefly, Mr Crosland's argument was this: the basis of most voting behaviour is class; the working class is shrinking, the middle class growing; therefore, in the long term, there will inevitably be an erosion of support from Labour, the working-class party, unless that party can change its image. And he concluded that the Liberal Party might well find itself a beneficiary of the withdrawal of support from Labour. 'Certainly,' wrote Mr Crosland, 'the pendulum will, for one reason or another, eventually swing against the Conservatives. But on the basis of recent voting trends it seems more likely to swing towards the Liberals and abstainers than towards Labour. The real danger is a 1924-type situation, with the Conservatives in a minority, but still able to rule because the majority is split between Liberals and Labour.'[25] Younger voters in particular, Mr Crosland believed, reacted especially strongly against Labour's class image and its 'identification with the problems and attitudes of a past generation'.[26]

Mr Crosland found considerable support for his analysis not only when he propounded it but subsequently when Liberal support in the country grew. For instance, Mr Geoffrey Rhodes, the Head of the Business Studies Department of a Lancashire Technical College, wrote after Orpington that the 'advance of the Liberals . . . represents a development quite fundamental to our social and political life—and the Labour Party must take account of this new factor in British politics or be ultimately replaced as the principal opposition party'. As a Labour candidate in the two previous general elections Mr Rhodes 'became convinced during the campaign that Labour would probably not win, because I constantly met people with an identical background to myself who would not vote Labour. These people were young professionals with parents of largely working-class background.'[27]

[25] C. A. R. Crosland, *Can Labour Win?* (Fabian Society, 1960), p. 4 reprinted in Crosland, *The Conservative Enemy* (1962), p. 145.

[26] Crosland, 'On the Left Again', *Encounter*, October 1960, reprinted in *The Conservative Enemy*, p. 128.

[27] G. Rhodes, 'Labour and the Young Professionals', *Socialist Commentary*, May 1962, p. 12.

Socialist Commentary agreed in a leading article[28] with Mr Rhodes. The Liberal revival, the magazine believed, reflected certain long-term currents of opinion in the country which might eventually prove very serious both for Labour and for the Conservatives. It would be a mistake, said *Socialist Commentary*, to conclude that, because the Liberal vote was not strongly rooted in any one of the traditional classes, it represented nothing more than a disgruntled assortment of people, bound soon to disintegrate as a political force because of its very rootlessness. Indeed Liberal supporters represented a new grouping with something of a new class-consciousness. They were the occupationally and socially mobile elements which were emerging in increasing numbers as the rigidities of the old class system broke down. 'These are the people with a chance to get on in their working and social lives and who want to make the most of that chance.'[29] Two months before this piece appeared the normally cautious psephologist Dr David Butler was moved to write that 'some new forces are plainly at work': the Liberals, fighting an assortment of seats found it almost impossible to drop below 20 per cent of the vote.[30]

A certain amount of support for the spin-drier school may be found in the small-sample survey which Dr Mark Abrams conducted.[31] Ten per cent of the sample refused to place themselves in any social class, usually on the ground that they did not believe in the class system. Two-thirds of the remainder described themselves as middle-class. It was unusual, said Dr Abrams, to find interviewees who were unwilling to pin class labels on themselves. Furthermore, Liberals who called themselves middle-class did so by reference not to income or family background but to occupation. This was 'something new in the English status system, and so far is mainly confined to people who claim to be Liberals'. As for the Liberals' view of their fellow Liberals, 40 per cent described them as middle-class and professional people, 35 per cent as voters dissatisfied with the other two parties and 18 per cent as young people. Despite this subjective identification of the Liberal Party with the middle-class, 34 per cent of Dr Abrams' sample were at-

[28] August 1962.
[29] ibid.
[30] *Sunday Times*, 27 May 1962.
[31] M. Abrams, 'Who are the New Liberals', *Observer*, 1 July 1962.

tracted to it by its 'classlessness'. Forty per cent were attracted to it because they were dissatisfied with the policies of the other two parties. While 16 per cent were attracted by the Liberals' 'virility and new ideas'.

The sample were united, however, in condemning the behaviour of work-people. In answer to a question about why British industrial production 'had been lagging', unofficial strikes, restrictive practices and too frequent demands for wage increases came in for particular censure. Moreover, there was considerable reluctance to agree that the country would have been better off with more governmental planning (though Dr Abrams is at pains to point out that Conservative and Labour supporters similarly placed this consideration at the bottom of the list). The survey found no backing for the theory that Liberal support sprang from personal economic frustration. Over the previous three or four years, 40 per cent said that they had done very well or fairly well, 32 per cent that they had held their own, 28 per cent that they had fallen back. 'On the basis of these figures,' concluded Dr Abrams, 'it would seem that among suburban voters the Liberals, better than either of the other parties, represent all classes; and further, because of their strong appeal to the young, the Liberals have in these areas a greater growth potential than the other two parties.'[32]

This, it should be remembered, was written in those heady days which followed Orpington. Even so, there is surely something a little unsatisfying in the explanations offered by the spin-drier school. Dr Abrams, of course, is a highly regarded political sociologist: but it is difficult to get rid of the impression that he may here be framing a hypothesis about society and then designing a questionnaire which may well bear that hypothesis out. Not only this: for Dr Abrams also seems committed to a particular view about the proper ends of political activity. 'There is a growing interest,' he once wrote, 'by the ordinary man and woman in local matters and local needs—schools, hospitals, town planning, roads, youth clubs, old people's clubs, smoke abatement, etc. Most of these are problems better tackled by professional skill rather than by ideological slogans, and this shift further encourages moderation and discourages extremism.'[33] The contrast between

[32] ibid.

[33] M. Abrams, 'British Electoral Behaviour', *Socialist Commentary*, May 1962, p. 12.

'professional skill' and 'ideological slogans', between 'moderation' and 'extremism', is hardly the most scientific form of phrasing that could be devised.[34]

Though Mr Crosland does not pretend to the exactitude of Dr Abrams, and though most of his writing was done before the Liberal revival attained its height, much the same applies to him. He too is committed to a particular view of present day politics: that the Labour Party should increasingly direct its appeal to a growing middle-class. With Mr Crosland's recommendations on Labour Party policy we are not here concerned: but they should be borne in mind in considering his social analysis.

There are broadly two questions. First, to what extent has a new middle-class emerged? Second, to what extent is this class voting Liberal?

As far as emergence is concerned, discussion is complicated by confusion among the objective idea of class, the subjective idea of class and the idea of status. Is the new middle-class accepted generally as such, particularly by members of the old middle-class? Or is it that the members of the new middle-class pin a label on themselves? Or do they perform jobs which carry a high status in the community? One answer which has been given to the first question is that 'the emphasis on deproletarianization is, in Great Britain at least, largely based on the undoubted increase in the prosperity of the working-class and the perpetuation by the British electorate of more than ten years of Conservative rule. But a bigger pay-packet does not automatically confer on a working-class man either the attitudes, or the speech, or the dress, or the recognition as an equal, of a different status-group. To assume, as some commentators seem to do, that whenever a factory worker buys a spin-drier or stops wearing a cloth cap or fails to vote Labour at a parliamentary election he is therefore motivated by the quest for status at the expense of traditional class loyalties is frankly absurd. David Lockwood has . . . made the essential point: "A washing-machine," as he puts it, "is a washing-machine is a washing-machine."[35] It might be objected by those

[34] From the present writer's knowledge of local authorities and their work: (i) It is not in general true that public interest in their activities is increasing. (ii) When, however, some matter does attract public attention, the tendency is for the parties to talk about principle and be less reluctant to settle the affair with the experts behind closed doors.

[35] W. G. Runciman, *Social Science and Political Theory* (1963), p. 143.

who are convinced of the emergence of this new class that Mr Runciman is casting his net too wide; that what is involved is not a more prosperous working-class but a fresh social group. Certainly it is easy to create a stereotype of a member of this group: pony tails and tartan trousers, a Span house, the *Guardian* on weekdays, the *Observer* on Sundays, *Which*? every month, and Dr Spock all the time. Clearly people who fit this (necessarily impressionistic) description do exist. Clearly, also, some of them vote Liberal. But what is not clear is why this grouping—to use the loosest word available—should be regarded as a particularly novel social phenomenon.[35a]

Above all, there is little to show that the Liberal Party has been a particularly favoured beneficiary. A special Gallup Poll inquiry into Liberal support[36] found there was no evidence whatsoever that Liberals represented any particular section of the community. This was true not only of objective classification but of subjective attitudes. The Liberals, according to the poll, retained the characteristic they had shown throughout the post-war period: of being the half-way house, the mid-point between the Conservatives and Labour. In respect of both objective and subjective attitudes, 'the Liberals today differ in no essential respect from Liberals, five, ten or even fifteen years ago'.[37] Naturally the detailed dissatisfactions of these Liberals were different. The poll listed the following issues on which opposition to the Government was noticeable: Mr Selwyn Lloyd's pay pause; fare increases; failure to give higher pensions to old people; failure to expand education; 'soft' handling of monopolists and take-overs; high mortgages and interest rates.

What is significant about this list, surely, is that on the whole the objections to the Government are not ones which would be made by a radical: the objections are of a standard middle-class variety. It is true, of course, that Dr Abrams found in his survey[38] that personal economic dissatisfaction played little part in the decision to vote Liberal. Nevertheless, two considerations should perhaps be borne in mind. First, people are always reluctant to admit, whether to interviewers or to anyone else, that they are

[35a] cf. J. Westergaard, 'The Withering Away of Class: a Contemporary Myth' in *Towards Socialism*, ed. P. Anderson and R. Blackburn (1965), p. 77.
[36] *Daily Telegraph*, 21 May 1962. [37] ibid.
[38] See above, pp. 24f.

worse off financially than they used to be. Second, at the height of the Liberal revival discontent was focused not so much on salary levels as on the cost of transport, the rate of mortgage repayment and, probably most important of all, the state of stagnation in the economy. In fact, as far as salaries are concerned, the middle-classes had held their own remarkably well. Between 1953 and 1960 wages per head rose by 49 per cent, salaries by 46 per cent. In the two years preceding October 1961 the weekly earnings of male adult manual workers increased by 13 per cent; the earnings of administrative, technical and clerical employees in the same group of industries went up by 11½ per cent. However, some particular expenses—house-purchase, for example—increased faster than the general rise in the cost of living. The price of a season-ticket from Orpington to London rose by more than 50 per cent in five years.[39]

It is not only the results of polls which confirm the impression that Liberal supporters, as distinct from the Liberal leadership, are not exactly of the Left (however broadly the Left may be defined). A study of election and by-election results leads broadly to the same conclusion. No one can reasonably think that Mr Eric Lubbock was voted in at Orpington, or Mr Mark Bonham Carter at Torrington, by radicals who were dissatisfied with the programme and policies of the Labour Party. Further, the Liberals' worst performances have been in constituencies where, on the face of it, they stood a good chance of defeating the Conservatives. They have done best in middle-class seats where the Labour threat was weak: thus a vote for the Liberal would not seriously affect the conservative candidates' chance of election. In general, the higher the Conservative majority, the higher the Liberal vote.[40] The clear implication of this is that the Liberal vote is an anti-Conservative vote, but not a radical one.

VII

It is an implication which raises a fundamental doubt as to Mr Grimond's decision on the position the Liberals should occupy in the political spectrum. For suppose Mr Grimond's decision had been different. Suppose he had made the Liberals a genuinely

[39] See S. Brittan in the *Observer*, 1 April 1962.
[40] A. J. Allen, *The English Voter* (1964), pp. 41, 67-8.

middle-of-the-road party, appealing to the prejudicies and interests of the middle classes. Suppose Mr Grimond—without embracing the attitudes of M. Poujade, or even of Mr Martell—had laid down that the object of the Liberals was to replace, not the Labour Party, but the Conservative. What would have happened then? Would we have witnessed a more impressive Liberal revival? Perhaps we would. But the question remains unprofitable. Mr Grimond is a man of definite political views who made a decision at a particular moment of time. It is doubtful whether, given the kind of man he is, he could have arrived at any other decision. More important, it is doubtful whether Mr Grimond—or even anyone else who happened to be leading the Liberal Party—could have carried the majority of the party activists with him in a centre party. Above all, a radical Liberal Party remains a political force. For a radical Liberal Party can combine with the Labour Party.

CHAPTER II

ANCESTRAL VOICES

In 1906 the Liberal Party returned 376 M.P.s; in 1951 it returned 6; today it returns a few more. During the twentieth century the picture presented by the figures is one of uniform decline, succeeded by a revival in the mid-1950's:[1]

Year	*No. of M.P.s*
1906	376
1910	270
1923	159
1929	59
1935	21
1945	12
1951	6

Yet figures can mislead, not so much because of any innate evil in arithmetic being applied to politics, as because entities with the same names are not necessarily the same entities. The Liberal Party of 1966 is different in such a degree from the Liberal Party of 1906 that the difference becomes one of kind: similarly with the Liberal Parties of 1906 and 1876. Mr G. Kitson Clark, the historian of the Conservative Party of the early nineteenth century, has questioned whether there is much continuum of doctrine in political parties;[2] naturally enough, the continuum has remained least broken—or most reverence has been paid to the past—in the most doctrinaire party, Labour; in this respect the Liberal Party has been closer to the Conservatives.

We can perceive this by taking three phases of the Liberal Party's existence: the mid-nineteenth century period, the early years of this century and the present day. The score or so years prior to the home rule split of 1886, and also the period 1906-16,

[1] These figures are taken from A. J. Allen, *The English Voter* (1964), p. 28. Other computations differ slightly: see e.g. Wilson Harris, 'The Plight of the Liberals', *Spectator*, 2 November 1951.

[2] G. Kitson Clark, *Peel and the Conservative Party* (1929), p. 214, quoted in S. H. Beer, *Modern British Politics* (1965), p. 250.

can be taken as successful times for the Liberal Party, if not always for Liberalism; while the last ten years, though not so glorious as the previous period, have provided convincing enough evidence that the Liberal Party still plays an important part in British politics.

The virtues of mid-Victorian Liberalism have been celebrated by writers as diverse as G. M. Young (who was in fact a Conservative), John Morley and Walter Bagehot. To Young, who, of course wrote many years after the other two, Liberalism was distinguished by its earnestness, its self-questioning, its extolling of production rather than consumption or distribution. Morley emphasised less its earnestness than its tolerance. Bagehot took a not so elevated, more detailed—if you like, more worldly-wise—stand than the other two. He was unlike them in attaching Liberalism firmly to an interest; he attached it to the rising middle-class, to the solid and the sensible; he invited us to smile with him at its illogicalities and inconsistencies;[3] nevertheless he left his readers in little doubt that, for England, the Liberal way was the right way.

It would be too much to say that there was a Liberal doctrine. There was, however, a Liberal body of thought; even a Liberal ideology, using 'ideology' in that extended sense so popular with modern sociologists. For those who like to see political philosophies embodied in individuals, Mr Enoch Powell is probably as good an exemplar as any of classical Liberalism. The phrase *laissez-faire* had better be avoided, as it has over the years gathered a thickish patina. It is less confusing to say that Liberalism, like Mr Powell, believed in the free play of market forces. This belief did not exclude a concurrent belief in State intervention in a limited class of cases: Mr Powell, for instance, believes that more money should be spent on prisons and mental hospitals, and less on free milk and orange juice—for which a perfectly respectable case can be made on Liberal or Conservative, as distinct from Socialist, premises. Nor, again, did a belief in the market exclude approval of libertarian reform.

It may appear somewhat arbitrary, to say the least, to take Mr Powell as the paradigm of pre-1886 Liberalism. Yet there is a good reason for doing so. For what we are considering here is theory and not practice; over the years, theories become more exact; the

[3] 'We may smile at . . .' was one of Bagehot's favourite phrases of patronage.

edges are sharpened and the moving parts are oiled; and Mr Powell is a more articulate spokesman for Gladstonian Liberalism than either Gladstone or Gladstone's disciple Morley. And in Gladstone we come to one of the central paradoxes of Liberalism. Of one thing we may be fairly sure: whatever else he may have been, at no stage of his life was he ever a Liberal. He began his political career as a placeman of the Duke of Newcastle, as Macaulay's rising hope of the stern, unbending Tories below the gangway. In his *Church and State* he supported the exclusion of the Jews from public office. Though his acute religious mania, of the High Church variety, persisted throughout his life—indeed, grew yet more maniacal with the passing of the years—he came to believe in freedom. He came also to believe in the People. But Gladstone's notion of freedom was entirely different from that of the classical Liberal. By 'freedom' Gladstone meant primarily the right of national groups to run their own affairs in their own way; in this respect, at least, Gladstone was one of the first of the Afro-Asians. Again, the People was not a concept which found any great favour with Liberal philosophers. It was, after all, a Tory Democrat's concept—something to which Lord Randolph Churchill was apt to appeal in moment of dialectical difficulty. The classical Liberal, such as Bagehot, was intensely suspicious of the People, in this being at one with Queen Victoria.

Nor was the non-Liberalism of the mid-nineteenth century Liberal Party demonstrated only in the person of Gladstone. One can perceive it in the composition of the party—this party of devout Christians and equally devout freethinkers, of high born Whigs and self made manufacturers, of grocers and gadflies.[3a] That all of these were not able to subscribe to all the tenets of Liberalism was not solely on account of their different interests; over and above these differences of interest there were different modes of thought; it is doubtful, for example, whether Morley ever fully understood Gladstone, or Gladstone Morley.

Again, if we examine the actual parliamentary disputes that were conducted in the pre-1886 period, we find that they were mostly about detailed questions of tariffs and taxation, or about foreign affairs. There was none of that opposition of rival political creeds which distinguished the inter-war or even the post-war

[3a] cf. J. Vincent, *The Formation of the Liberal Party 1857-1868* (1966), which appeared after this chapter had been written.

years of this century. The Liberal conscience was seen to its best advantage in movements with an extra-parliamentary basis—such as the protest against the measure to introduce compulsory medical examination of prostitutes in garrison towns.

And yet, having admitted all this, it must still be recognized that there was in existence a body of Liberal principles to which politicians could and did appeal. (Gladstone, on the other hand, was fond of appealing to the Christian conscience of Europe.) However, as the nineteenth century drew to its close, these principles became more and more cloudy and were appealed to less and less.

Why was this? Possibly because Gladstone went on for too long: if Dilke had emerged as his political heir at an earlier stage, and if Dilke had not become involved with the courts as he did, if this and many other things had happened, the history of the Liberal Party in the last quarter of the nineteenth century would have been different. And yet Dilke, the author of *Greater Britain*, was an Imperialist, and it was imperialism as much as anything which divided the Liberal Party.

We had better look for explanations less in the fate of particular politicians, and more in the acceptance of general ideas. Imperialism, as a political notion, was tied to the elevation of finance over production. It was tied also to a lessening of what can only be called political seriousness. The failure to provide quickly enough an adequate system of secondary education—G. M. Young's great complaint against the nineteenth century—was both a cause and an effect of this break-down in the machinery of political discussion. The split over home rule was not the beginning of the Liberal decline but the visible sign of the Liberal end.

The party which took office in 1906 was, somehow, coarser-textured. It was, to be sure, full of exuberant men, notably Churchill and Lloyd George: one of their main characteristics as a pair was that neither of them was a Liberal. If Churchill is to be called anything, Tory Radical is probably the name which fits best. Lloyd George likewise was a Radical, but an agrarian Radical from North Wales. He was obsessed by landlords; not the landlords of the big cities but the land-owners of the North Wales of his youth. He neither liked nor understood modern industrial society.[4] The 1906 Liberal Government, we have been told often

[4] See K. O. Morgan, *Lloyd George: Welsh Radical as World Statesman* (1963).

enough, laid the foundations of the Welfare State, and so of course it did, with disastrous results for the future: for the present absurd ritual of stamp sticking is a legacy not only of Beveridge but also of Lloyd George. It is difficult to perceive any intellectual consistency in the performance of the Liberal Government of before the first world war. Like Disraeli, it was interested in amelioration—a splendid cry, as Tadpole observed to Taper. Apart from various measures of amelioration, the administrations of Campbell-Bannerman and Asquith were distinguished by several acts of petty persecution designed to appease various narrow interests. Examples are provided by the Licensing Bill and the Education Bill and the Bill to disestablish the Welsh Church.

One does not want to be churlish about the achievements of the post-1906 Liberal governments: but matters must be put into perspective. However, worse was to follow, with the quarrels between the Asquithites and the Lloyd Georgites and later between the Samuelites and the Simonites. Yet a party can survive quarrels, if its heart is strong enough. This was demonstrated by Labour after MacDonald had joined the National Government. It was demonstrated again during the Bevanite period, and subsequently in the Clause IV controversy. While the Conservatives, for their part, survived both Suez and the accession of Sir Alec Douglas-Home. Certainly personal disagreements played their part in the inter-war decline of the Liberal Party: but they are not the whole story.

Did the Liberal Party decline then, because it ceased adequately to represent an interest—the working-class?[5] The question can be included in a wider one: is it necessary for a modern political party to represent an interest? Mr Grimond asked this question and replied: 'It need not—indeed cannot—be based on an interest in the old simple sense. Instead of digging themselves into the class and interest structure people are in various ways trying to break out of it. Culture is more general. Television is a great leveller. Status symbols are more universal. The economic divisions are altering. It is the middle rank of university teachers, workmen in certain towns of high unemployment, some small farmers, who feel the economic pinch, and these are not an homogeneous interest. The young less than ever want to take on their parents' clothes,

[5] cf. R. Rose 'How the Party System Works' in M. Abrams and Rose, *Must Labour Lose?* (1960), p. 71.

real or figurative'.[6] Mr Grimond is here talking about the late 1950's and the early 1960's, but a similar conclusion can be reached, by a different route, in respect of the inter-war period. For the outstanding characteristics of the British political system are these: first (which is familiar enough) that it is not based on ethnic or religious differences; secondly (and this is less familiar) that economic or other interest plays a minor part in the voting pattern. Let us put this slightly differently: the surprising thing is that Britain has, and always has had, such a strong Conservative Party and such a weak Communist Party. However the working-class is defined, one discovers that a substantial minority votes Conservative.[7] We need not concern ourselves at the moment with the reasons why this is so: let us merely observe that 'interest' is not a conclusive determinant of voting behaviour in Britain.

It may be noted that in much current political literature the word interest is used in at least two distinct, though not opposing, senses. First, it is used of a broad socio-economic grouping—such as land, labour, the working-classes, the middle-classes, the young technicians, the new competitors, Orpington man, or what you will—which expresses its wants and aspirations through a political party. Second, 'interest' is used of a narrower grouping—such as the farmers, the doctors, the motorists, the huntsmen, the anti-huntsmen—which proceeds by means of a pressure organization.

Liberals have for a long time been proud that their party has been remote from interest, in either of the above senses of the word. As Sir William Beveridge put it, 'The outstanding merit of Liberalism as a political creed—that it stands for the general interest—means that the Liberal Party, unlike both its rivals, cannot count on automatic support from any sectional interest. It must build its own organization for itself and its ideals'.[8] Mr Grimond, on the other hand—and despite his views on interest given above—believes that 'it is not "dishonest" for a politician to put forward the point of view of some group. Liberals have far too often ignored the group. Individuals have not the capacity or the energy to think continually for themselves'.[9] Again, Mr Grimond has written that 'politics must have regard to conflicts. There are con-

[6] J. Grimond, *The Liberal Challenge* (1963), pp. 312-13.

[7] Unless, of course, the working class is defined in terms of non-Conservative voting.

[8] Sir W. Beveridge, *Why I am a Liberal* (1945), p. 15.

[9] Grimond, op. cit. p. 48.

flicts between classes, between pressure groups, between rulers and ruled. Conflicts can be necessary to liberty. Liberals should not condemn all pressure groups, for instance. Such groups are only damaging when they grow too big like a cancer or, like a weed, choke more useful developments.'[10] It is clear that in both these passages Mr Grimond is using the word interest in its second, narrower sense. There is therefore no conflict with the passage first quoted, in which he denies, on the whole rightly, that interest is essential as a basis to a political party.

If we are looking for an explanation for the Liberal Party's decline in the years prior to and immediately following the last war, the facts of the electoral system are at least as important as the questions of interest-representation. Though it is true, as Mr Grimond has pointed out,[11] that the British system has never been a two-party one, it is at the same time true that electoral arrangements tend to maintain the dominance of two parties. If M.P.s are elected from single-member constituencies by means of a simple majority, a third party will inevitably find itself in a naturally declining position, for the reason that the majority of electors are reluctant to 'waste their vote'. In 1906 the Liberal Party was elected with a vast parliamentary majority; while by 1924 the party had fewer than one tenth of the seats in the House of Commons. Such a decline was due, not to any catastrophic fall in the appeal of the party's leadership or programme, but to the fact that the Liberals had been made the 'third party'. From this point the party was at a disadvantage.[12]

There is, however, one exception to this tendency of third parties to decline. This exception is the Irish Party. There are several reasons for this. For one thing, the Irish drew their support from a defined electoral area. For another, they concentrated their attentions upon one particular grievance. But, above all, the Irish were more gifted and resourceful parliamentarians. For the failure of the Liberals, at least in the immediate post war period, was as much a parliamentary failure as anything.

Yet, as Dr Richard Rose observes, 'The Conservative and Labour Parties do not have a freehold claim on the party system.

[10] ibid. p. 133.

[11] ibid. p. 309.

[12] See R. Rose, 'How the Party System Works' in Abrams and Rose, op. cit. pp. 55-60. See also W. G. Runciman, *Social Science and Political Theory* (1963), p. 106.

To assume that they do is either to suggest that the electorate is incapable of change or that politicians are infinitely flexible in responding to electoral demands. The electors today are not doomed to oscillate eternally between the Conservative and Labour parties. These two parties seem to hold their positions on indefinite lease—terminable at the pleasure of the electorate.'[13]

For a time—in 1960-62—it was possible that Labour would become the 'third party', with all that implies electorally.[14] This did not happen, for reasons that are discussed later in this book. It will probably never happen. The Labour Party has sufficient reserves of voting strength to enable it to maintain its position as one of the two major parties. And yet, for all kinds of reasons, Labour and the Liberals are likely to draw closer together. The only purpose of this chapter is to suggest that, whether one is judging the likelihood or the desirability of such a drawing closer, history is an unsure guide and the ancestral voices speak in an uncertain tone. Political parties, in short, change; they do not represent the same interests as they did even thirty years ago; and the only guide to political action lies in moral judgement about the exigencies of the present.

[13] R. Rose 'How the Party System Works' in Abrams and Rose, op. cit. p. 59.

[14] See S. M. Lipset in *Socialist Commentary*, March 1961. He wrote that 'if this split (in the Labour Party) were to widen and eventually lead to the party's collapse then a new Opposition will eventually arise to take its place. But in this article I am not dealing with extremities.' To which Mr Arthur Holt replied in the *Guardian* of 3 March 1961: 'Extremities indeed! The widening split in the Labour Party is THE great reality of British Party politics today. If anyone doubted it they can hardly do so after the bitter public row which broke out this week over defence between Mr Crossman and the supporters of Mr Gaitskell.'

CHAPTER III

THE CONSERVATIVE SYREN SONG

IN what, precisely, did the Liberal Party believe in 1945? 'Ah, in those days,' Lady Megan Lloyd George once told the present writer, 'in those days we were a Radical party.' At first sight the claim may appear strange. It does not quite fit the mental pattern which many have formed of the history of the modern Liberal Party: a pattern of ever-increasing radicalism, broadening down from Sir Archibald Sinclair through Clement Davies to Mr Jo Grimond.

And, yet, at the 1945 election, the Liberal manifesto was surprisingly leftist both in content and in tone. On housing, for instance, the Liberals declared that they would not be satisfied until there was a separate dwelling for each family at a reasonable rent. This could be achieved only by a completely new approach 'applying to housing the same drive as was used to produce aircraft and munitions of war'.[1] No vested interests could be allowed to stand in the way, and the cost of building materials should be controlled. As for the related question of land, development rights outside built-up areas should be acquired for the public. There should be a periodic levy on all increases in site values; and every increase in value that was due to community action should be secured for the community.

Nor was nationalization spurned. Coal should be 'a public service': transport and power should be organized as public utilities. The principle laid down was that where public ownership was more economic, Liberals would demand it without hesitation. When there was no further expansion or useful competition in an industry, or when it had become a private monopoly, then it should be nationalized. It is little wonder that Lady Megan was

[1] Which recalls the reply Aneurin Bevan once made, when Minister of Health, to an unfriendly questioner who demanded that housing should be treated 'as a military operation.' 'But the whole point is,' said Bevan, 'that we are not engaged in a military operation. If we were I could have troublesome people like you sh-sh-shot.'

by and large satisfied with the radicalism of the Liberal Party at this time.

Of course, one must not exaggerate the Liberals' radicalism. On administrative tribunals, for example, the party's only remedy was to go back to the recommendations of the Committee on Ministers' Powers, 1932: but, as neither of the major parties considered the problems of the executive State worth thinking about, still less worth mentioning, the Liberals can scarcely be blamed for advocating nineteenth century solutions to an essentially twentieth century problem. On free trade, again, there were echoes of an older attitude: at the Assembly of February 1945 the party re-affirmed its support for free trade 'as tending to preserve peace among the nations, to maintain employment and a high standard of living, and generally to promote the prosperity and happiness of the community'.[2] In general, however, Liberal policy was more radical than it was subsequently to become; and it is worth asking why this should have been so.

First, of course, there was the mood of the time, a mood which is difficult to recapture fully today. It was the age of CEMA concerts and Dr Joad on the Brains Trust; it was the age when the service education officer came into his own; it was an age which still believed in progress. Second, there was the influence on the party of Radical Action, a group of youngish Liberals, including Miss Honor Balfour and Mr Dingle Foot, who had been active in propagating leftish ideas in the years prior to 1945. Third, and above all, there was Sir William Beveridge.

It is not too much to say that what Churchill was to the Conservatives, Beveridge was to the Liberals. His report *Full Employment in a Free Society* provided the party, for the first time since the days of the Yellow Book and 'we can conquer unemployment', with a popular issue to put before the electorate. Beveridge became a member of the Liberal Party in July 1944: he had not done so earlier because he had considered membership inconsistent with his roles of civil servant and university teacher.[3] In October 1944 he succeeded George Grey, the Liberal M.P. for Berwick-on-

[2] Quoted Sir W. Beveridge, *Why I am a Liberal* (1945), p. 114. And cf. Sir A. Sinclair at the Liberal Party Council, reported *The Times*, 30 May 1945.

[3] R. S. Sommer, The Organization of the Liberal Party 1937-60, a thesis in the library of the London School of Economics and Political Science, p. 74. I have found Mr Sommer's work particularly valuable on the period 1945-51.

Tweed, who was killed in action. The *Guardian*[4] commented: 'Parliament and the Liberal Party will be richer, though not the quieter, for Sir William Beveridge. An administrator and teaching economist for most of his life, he has become at 65 the people's man, first the prophet and not the protector of their social hopes. It is not perhaps an exaggeration to suggest that his name stands for as much in the domestic field as Churchill's does in the sphere of war.'

Sir William set himself firmly against *laissez-faire*. The necessaries of civilized life, he said, could not be secured by individuals: they had to be won by collective planning and social demand. None of the Liberal leaders from Gladstone onwards had stood for *laissez-faire*; and if the party was thought to stand for *laissez-faire* in 1945 it would have no chance at the polls, and would deserve no chance. Nor was Sir William necessarily opposed to State enterprise: the officials of an insurance company or a railway company, he wrote, were the true bureaucrats, because if one had a grievance there was often no recourse against them. A State official was less of a bureaucrat because questions about him could always be asked in Parliament. In short, Sir William believed that 'Liberalism with a Radical programme means not interfering with rights, but giving additional rights: I suggest that every housewife in this country shall have a right to a tap'.[5]

He began his election tour at Hereford on 25 May 1945. He worked his way down the West Country to Cornwall and returned via Oxford. He spoke in Liverpool on 13 June and crossed Cheshire and North Wales during the next few days. A week later he toured Scotland. And before polling day he visited Yorkshire. 'His travels in the service of his party,' commented Dr McCallum and Miss Readman, 'were particularly praiseworthy in that it was well known that his seat was shaky, and he could ill afford to be so long away from Berwick.'[6] Of Sir William's performance in Edinburgh Miss Readman wrote: 'More than a thousand citizens had forgathered there to hear him, as their fathers had gathered to hear Mr Gladstone. They gave him the same alert, respectful attention that they would have accorded Mr Gladstone, but it

[4] 15 October 1944.

[5] Sir W. Beveridge, speeches at Oxford, Newcastle and the Liberal Assembly, reprinted Beveridge, *Why I am a Liberal* (1945), pp. 29, 30, 37, 66.

[6] R. B. McCallum and A. Readman, *The British General Election* of 1945 (1946), p. 136.

was not Gladstonian oratory that they were to hear. As Sir William drew near the end of a closely reasoned discourse on social security, lasting peace and full employment in a free society, which he had sustained for almost an hour, concentration seemed perceptibly to ease. Nevertheless he sat down amidst enthusiastic applause. One could not but feel, however, that the old fire of Liberalism, which had burned so ardently during the great days of the Midlothian campaign, was now almost extinct. It was an emasculated heritage into which the three Liberal candidates were entering. Their birthright was eluding them.'[7]

As far as his own special subject was concerned, Sir William maintained that the government's social insurance proposals would not abolish want: the provisions for family allowances and old age pensions were inadequate. He proposed a minimum of nine shillings for every child after the first, and a pension of thirty-five shillings as of right. And he did not trust the coalition government's intentions on full employment.[8]

As campaign chairman, Beveridge had only a month in which to find candidates and money and to fight a campaign. Whether the Liberals would have done better if the election had been fought somewhat later is difficult to say. At least the Liberals thought so, though it should be remembered that political parties on the losing side invariably claim that they would have done better if the election had been held at some different time. The Liberal leader, Sir Archibald Sinclair, expressed a preference for an autumn election[9] which would enable the party to fight on the October electoral register. Sir Archibald, like Mr Attlee, believed that this would work to the advantage of the non-Conservative parties.

After the election had taken place in July some Liberals blamed its timing for the party's failure to put forward the hoped-for 500 candidates. Three hundred and seven were fielded, and only twelve were returned, eight fewer than in the previous parliament. True, two seats were gained from the Conservatives, and one from Labour: but this was small consolation for the defeats of Sir Archibald Sinclair in Caithness and Sir William Beveridge in Berwick-on-Tweed. Lady Violet Bonham Carter was equally unsuccessful. All in all, 1945 was a Liberal massacre.

[7] ibid. p. 166. [8] ibid. p. 64.
[9] *The Times*, 22 May 1945.

The Liberals had asked for the support of the voters primarily on the grounds that they were the party best fitted to put the Beveridge proposals into practice and that they had no 'vested interests' or 'axe to grind'. The voters were unimpressed. 'Electors,' comment Dr McCallum and Miss Readman, 'like their votes to count one way or another; they do not like to feel that they are casting waste paper into the ballot box. This was disastrous to the Liberals.'[10] A Mass Observation Report of June 1945 showed that while there was basic goodwill towards the Liberals, there was also a strong feeling that to vote for them would be to waste a vote.[11] The party itself, in a post-election statement issued from headquarters, said that it had suffered a reverse as overwhelming as it was unexpected. Reports from the constituencies had shown almost without exception a keener interest in the Liberal programme than for many years. However, it was clear that the majority of electors were mainly concerned to defeat the Conservative Party. Liberal candidates were rejected not because the voters disapproved of their policy but because they appeared to offer a less effective alternative.[12]

A few months before the election, four officers of the Oxford University Liberal Club had written to Beveridge, making six points on the survival of the party. These were:

(i) Negotiations should be re-opened with the National Liberals.

(ii) Sir Archibald Sinclair and Sir William Beveridge should immediately seek re-election to Parliament.

(iii) The Liberal Party should not try to be an alternative government, but only an 'energetic though small force in the political life of the nation'.

(iv) The party should not fight more than a hundred carefully chosen seats in the election.

(v) There should be a thorough reorganization of the party machine in London and in the country.

(vi) Candidates should either support agreed policy or leave the party.[13]

After the election Miss Joan de Robeck, the acting secretary of

[10] McCallum and Readman, op. cit. p. 118.

[11] Mass Observation Ltd., Report No. 2259, June 1945, quoted Sommer thesis, p. 78.

[12] *The Times*, 1 August 1945.

[13] The four were Arnold Hever (President), Alan Gibson, Keith Dewhurst and Pamela Brisbane (ex-President). Sommer thesis, pp. 85-6.

the Women's Liberal Federation, blamed the disaster on the lack of speakers, or agents and of organization; she talked of '. . . completely green candidates . . . working with agents quite as green as themselves'.[14] And Mr (as he then was) Roy Harrod, the candidate for Huddersfield, saw the election as a repudiation of a middle of the road party in Britain. He said—anticipating Mr Grimond—that if the Liberal Party were to survive it would have to become the alternative progressive party.[15]

Following the defeat of Sir Archibald Sinclair, the party had to find a new leader; and the choice fell upon Clement Davies, member for Montgomery and a prosperous lawyer. At the same time a reconstruction committee was appointed to study organization and make recommendations for its improvement.[16] The committee said that unlike their predecessors of the Meston Commission (who had presented in 1936 the reorganization report which had given the party its constitution) they had been unable to conclude that '"Liberalism has now passed through its worst trials and survived them, and that its revival is as assured as it is necessary." On the contrary, we have been forced to realize that the world is faced with the possible eclipse of British Liberalism.' Broadly, the committee concluded that inspiration and energy should be drawn from the national organization into the centre and hence redistributed throughout the country, the area federations making the necessary local adaptations and adjustments. The party should not be identified with its headquarters, which was only a part of the whole.[17]

More important, perhaps, were the committee's recommendations on finance. In the Liberal Party money was a delicate topic: it was connected with questions of party democracy and of the position the party should take up in the political spectrum. As the reconstruction committee put it, 'the central office of the party has depended upon annual subscriptions and contributions collected by the treasurers from a comparatively limited circle of

[14] J. de Robeck, Confidential Report on Problems Arising from the General Election, dated 13 July 1945, quoted Sommer thesis, p. 85.

[15] R. Harrod, *Lessons of the Election* (Liberal Publications Department, 1945), quoted Sommer thesis, p. 89.

[16] The committee's members were: Noel Newsome; Philip Fothergill; Frank Byers, M.P.; Mrs. Doreen Gorrky; A. J. F. Macdonald; Lawrence Maitland; Paul Wright; and Mrs. Ethel Wood.

[17] *Coats off for the Future*, p. 5, quoted Sommer thesis, p. 89.

generous subscribers.'[18] Harcourt Johnston, Lord (Jimmy) de Rothschild and Lord Sherwood had for many years been generous. And Lord Snowden both contributed and publicly encouraged others to do so,[19] 'Representatives of subscribers'—there were five, elected by the rest of the donors—were given a special position on the Liberal Council. Politically they were well to the right. The reconstruction committee recommended the establishment of a fund-raising body. This body was set up even before the Assembly had considered the Report. It was placed in the hands of Mr Edward Martell. His schemes included a foundation fund, foundation day activities, the establishment of the *Liberal News* and a bequest system under which people could give money to the party. He raised the party's income to its highest point since 1936. 'How,' the present writer once inquired of Mr Martell, 'do you get people to give you money?' 'I ask them for it,' he replied. However, disagreements developed between Mr Martell and the Executive. Clashes of personality were as much as anything responsible. Mr Martell believed that the Executive were trying to interfere in his projects; the Executive felt that Mr Martell was spending too much money in an effort to collect more. Mr Martell finally left the party.

The dominating issue of this period, however, was not finance or internal organization or even policy. It was the degree to which the Liberal Party should assist the Conservatives (whether voluntarily or otherwise). And it must be recorded of Clement Davies that, though many members of the party considered him altogether too inclined towards the right, he resisted all the Conservative approaches. To understand the story it is necessary to go back briefly to 1931, when a group of twenty-five M.P.s detached themselves from the Liberal Party and became allied to the Conservatives. They adopted the title of Liberal National, which was changed to National Liberal in 1948. On several occasions during the war discussions took place between representatives of the Liberal Party and of the Liberal Nationals. The discussions concluded with the Liberal Party issuing this statement on 5 October 1944: 'It is the intention of the Liberal Party at the next general election to put forward, without any commitments to any other party, the largest possible number of its own candidates, in complete independence, presenting the party's independent pro-

[18] *Coats off for the Future*, p. 38.
[19] *Glasgow Herald*, 8 October 1936, quoted Sommer thesis, p. 96.

gramme.' On 20 November 1944 was published a letter from Sir Archibald Sinclair to Ernest Brown of the Liberal Nationals. Sir Archibald said that the Liberal Party considered it was in the interests of the country, and of the proper working of democratic government, that the principal issues of policy which the next Parliament had to decide should be presented to the people by political parties acting independently of one another. Brown replied: 'Our common conclusions that joint action is not now possible is the more disappointing because the discussions on policy had gone a considerable way towards agreement. I must, however, not overlook the fact that the tendency to seek association exclusively with Socialists, which has shown itself in your party, would be inconsistent with the forthright presentation of the case for liberty, in accordance with Liberal beliefs, upon which all Liberal Nationals are resolved.'[20]

Co-operation between the Liberals and the Liberal Nationals, then, was in the highest degree unlikely. But co-operation between the Liberal Nationals and the Conservatives? This was an altogether more promising enterprise. In May 1947 Lord Woolton, the chairman of the Conservative Party, arrived at an agreement with Lord Teviot of the Liberal Nationals. This provided as follows: First, in constituencies where each party already had an organization, a combined association should be formed under a mutually agreed title which indicated their community of purpose. Second, in constituencies where only one of the parties had an organization, that organization should consider including in its membership all those who supported joint action against Socialism; and the title should be extended accordingly. Third, in constituencies where combined associations were looking for a candidate a joint list would, if requested, be prepared by both party headquarters in consultation. Fourth, combined association would be eligible for affiliation both to the National Union of Conservatives and Unionist Associations and to the National Liberal Council. And, lastly, in constituencies where a combined organization had been formed it was suggested that the most suitable designation for the prospective candidate would be 'Liberal and Unionist'.[21] In May 1949 Woolton said there were sixty constituencies in which a joint Conservative-Liberal Association would

[20] Supplement to the 7th Annual Report to the Assembly (1944), pp. 9-10.
[21] See *Who are the National Liberals?* (1951), p. 8.

sponsor a joint candidate.[22] In most of these constituencies the separate National Liberal and Conservative associations were dissolved and a joint association of both set up. In the remainder the separate associations were preserved, but unity between them brought about by the establishment of a joint committee representative of both.[23]

Britain, Lords Woolton and Teviot had said in a joint statement, was facing a difficult and dangerous situation. There was, they declared, 'a widespread determination in the country that the British people must be saved from a further period of Socialist misgovernment. There is also a growing realization that this objective transcends all considerations of narrower party interests, and that it can only be achieved if all the forces opposed to Socialism are effectively united.'[24] The Liberals replied by saying that, in all parts of the country, Conservative Central Office was pursuing a deliberate, carefully thought out campaign to undermine Liberal organizations. In most areas this campaign took the shape of an informal approach in the first place to a well-known local Liberal, in the hope that he would exert his influence to persuade fellow Liberals to join in the formation of an anti-Socialist front. The reply went on to call upon 'all Liberals throughout the country to stand firm against Conservative overtures and to concentrate all their energies upon preparing for the coming fight'.[25]

Further details were provided by Sir Andrew McFadyean. He disclosed that in November 1948, a meeting was held at Dunstable in private, with only invited persons present. The prospective Liberal candidate and some members of the local Liberal association were refused admittance to the meeting, which set up a 'United Liberal and Conservative Association'. Again, in December 1948 a meeting was convened in Kirriemuir to consider a merger between the local Liberal and Unionist Associations. A handful of Unionists attended; there were no Liberals present. The merger was approved by not a single Liberal. Another example was provided by the North Angus constituency, where in February 1949 a meeting was attended by five hundred Conservatives and three

[22] H. G. Nicholas, *The British General Election of 1950* (1951), pp. 82-3.
[23] *Who are the National Liberals?* (1951), p. 10.
[24] Statement of 9 May 1947, reprinted ibid. p. 8.
[25] *The Times*, 27 November 1947.

Liberals, steps having been taken deliberately to exclude Liberals in general. The three who had managed to get in were asked to leave when they voiced their objections to a merger. Similarly, in March 1949 all Liberals 'interested' were invited to attend a meeting of the 'Torrington Division United Liberal and Conservative Association (Bideford area)'. The chairman, the secretary and some members of the Liberal Association did in fact attend. They were informed in reply to a question that 'Liberal' had been incorporated in the title as a result of a decision taken at an earlier meeting which had been attended by no Liberals. When she protested, the secretary of the local Liberal Association was told either to keep quiet or to leave the hall. She left, accompanied by about twenty other Liberals.[26]

Not surprisingly, these arrangements sometimes caused confusion in the minds of the voters. This, after all, was part of their object. But the confusion did not invariably work to the Conservatives' advantage. At Luton Dr Charles Hill (as he then was) stood as a 'Liberal and Conservative' candidate. Two days before the election he clearly felt it necessary to say what this meant. 'There is absolutely no truth,' went a statement 'in the story being put out by canvassers in the division that I am an Independent Liberal. I am, in fact, being opposed by an Independent Liberal. I am a United Liberal-Conservative candidate, representing both Liberal and Conservative opinion. I would also like to make it clear that I am not a National Liberal.'[27]

The Woolton-Teviot agreement and its consequences should be distinguished from the genuine attempts that had been made to secure co-operation between the Liberals and the Conservatives. Owing to the interest which Churchill, the ex-Liberal, continued to take in the party, there was always the possibility, however slender, that this co-operation might come about. The possibility was at intervals mooted in news stories and articles; and as early as 1946 Liberal headquarters issued a statement, in the names of Lady Violet Bonham Carter (the president of the party organization) and Philip Fothergill (the chairman of the executive), denying a story of a Liberal-Conservative pact.[28]

[26] Letter, ibid. 21 November 1949. But see letter by John Maclay, ibid. 24 November 1949.
[27] Quoted Nicholas, op. cit. p. 107.
[28] *The Times*, 18 November 1946.

Four months later Churchill made an approach. He asked Lady Rhys Williams to put a proposal for co-operation before a number of leading Liberals. If the response was favourable, he would put the proposal to his fellow-Conservatives. The offer was based on the complete independence of both parties, though the Conservatives would have a policy broadly similar to that contained in the Liberal manifesto. In return for a promise of parliamentary support, the Conservatives would withdraw in a number of constituencies. This offer was conveyed by Lady Rhys Williams to the president of the party, the chairman of the executive, the chairman of the organization committee and other notables. However, the response was unfavourable: almost immediately the party promised to put up 600 candidates at the next election. 'In spite of this rebuff,' wrote Lady Rhys Williams, 'I again approached the new president of the party, following the Liberal Council meeting in September 1947, and put the whole matter to him afresh; but without result.' It was certainly surprising, she wrote, that these approaches should not have been reported to the party committee by any of the leaders concerned.[29] It appears here that Lady Rhys Williams was in error. The Liberal Party committee was fully informed. It was told at a meeting in the House of Commons on 27 October 1947, presided over by the Chief Whip, Mr Frank Byers. The proposals were submitted by a Liberal group of which Mr Douglas Mitchell was chairman; and they were discussed at a further meeting of the Liberal committee.[30]

But nothing came of Churchill's idea. Indeed, looking back it is surprising that Conservative overtures were rejected with such near-unanimity. Surprising because, under Clement Davies, the party had shifted to the right.[31] Policy struck a less radical note than that of 1945; and in the parliamentary party there was a fundamental conflict between those who wanted the Liberals to be basically anti-Socialist and those—the remnants of the Radical Action group—who wanted the party to be basically anti-Tory. Yet the anti-Socialists, who, on the whole, won this conflict, resisted all Conservative approaches, which continued until the election, and persisted after it.

[29] Letter ibid. 13 February 1950.

[30] Letter from Douglas K. Mitchell, ibid. 15 February 1950.

[31] Mr Sommer, in his valuable thesis, disagrees with this assessment; the present writer, however, has the consolation that Lady Megan Lloyd George agreed with him.

Though the schemes for a legitimate, or legitimatised, alliance between the Conservatives and the Liberals came to nothing, this did not inhibit Central Office from making the fullest use of the Woolton-Teviot agreement. A statement by Churchill and Lord Rosebery (the president of the National Liberal Council) advised that, in constituencies where joint associations had been formed, candidates should stand as 'Liberal-Conservatives' or 'Liberal-Unionists', adding the word 'National' where a 'left-wing' Liberal was standing.[32] This statement followed a letter from Lord Moynihan, the chairman of the Liberal Party Organization, to Lord Woolton. Lord Moynihan said that 'Conservative candidates should fight the election as Conservatives and that the name "Liberal" should not be used by them in order to confuse the issue.'[33]

'I should indeed be glad,' replied Woolton, 'to do anything that would assist in clarifying the position with which the voters of this country are faced. I do not think that your object would be achieved by your suggestion that the use of the word "Liberal" should be confined to those whose candidatures are sponsored by your organization. In fact, this would have the opposite effect, of misleading the public. The National Liberals are at least as entitled to the label "Liberal" as those others on whose behalf you write. In the House of Commons the National Liberals are numerically stronger than the Liberals led by Mr Clement Davies. There is also in the country a large body of electors who have sacrificed nothing of their Liberal principles by endorsing the policy of co-operation with the Conservatives against Socialism. This policy has found expression in the adoption in more than sixty constituencies of candidates who combine the support and the names of both parties.'[34]

This reply was hardly calculated to assuage the Liberal Party; nor did it. Legal action was threatened against the Conservatives; and Clement Davies wrote to Churchill.[35] 'As you were yourself for eleven years a National Liberal,' replied Churchill, 'and in that capacity supported the Governments of Mr Baldwin and Mr Neville Chamberlain, I should not presume to correct

[32] *The Times*, 23 January 1950.
[33] Nicholas, op. cit. p. 83.
[34] *The Times*, 21 January 1950.
[35] See Nicholas, op. cit. pp. 84-5 and *The Times*, 24 and 25 January 1950.

your knowledge of the moral, intellectual and legal aspects of adding a prefix or a suffix to the honoured name of Liberal. . . Since, however, you have been good enough to address me, I will venture to draw your attention to the fact that you and your friends do not seem to have any difficulty on the question of nomenclature with the Socialist Party. I have not heard, for instance, of any candidate who is standing as a Liberal-Socialist. The reason is, no doubt, that the two terms are fundamentally incompatible . . . Why, then, should you and your friends and your four hundred candidates always blame the Conservative Party, and do all in your power to help the Socialists?'[36]

Davies put pen to paper a second time. 'I have received your reply,' he wrote to Churchill. 'I am sorry that, on a matter of such public importance, it should appear to be, and is evidently intended to be, facetious and evasive. In my letter I set out the facts in four specific instances where so-called Liberal-Conservative associations were set up without the participation of a single member of the Liberal Party, and asked whether, when these facts were brought to your attention, you would still be prepared to lend your great name and the high prestige of your position to the perpetration of a calculated deception. I gather that, knowing those facts, you are, nevertheless, prepared to support and approve what we Liberals regard as an unworthy subterfuge.'[37]

In his adoption speech at Woodford on 20 January 1950 Churchill returned to the attack, talking of 'the very small and select group of Liberal leaders who conceived themselves the sole heirs of the principles and traditions of Liberalism, and believed themselves to have the exclusive copyright of the word "Liberal".' And so it went on, with accusations and counter-accusations flying merrily to and fro. There is little doubt that most of the right lay on the Liberal side.

However, the announcement of the Huddersfield agreement detracted a little from the absolute purity of the Liberals' protestations. Under this agreement the Conservatives agreed not to fight the West Huddersfield constituency, while the Liberals agreed not to fight the East. The Conservatives asked Mr Donald Wade, the Liberal nominee in the West, for an undertaking that if the Liberals held the balance of power in parliament he would 'vote

[36] Quoted Nicholas, op. cit. pp. 85-6.
[37] *The Times*, 27 January 1950.

against a vote of confidence in a Socialist administration'. Mr Wade said that he would not enter into a bargain, but that he certainly 'would not vote in such a way as to give a vote of confidence to an administration committed to further Socialist measures'. 'Mr Wade,' responded the Conservatives, 'has given the undertaking for which we asked'. Whereupon they withdrew their candidate, and Liberal headquarters endorsed the Huddersfield formula.[38]

Subsequently the Liberals appealed to Conservative Associations which were intending to oppose existing Liberal M.P.s: the Conservatives were asked to withdraw rather than create a situation from which Labour might benefit. The same applied to other constituencies such as Bethnal Green which, in the Liberal view, could be won from Labour only by Sir Percy Harris. The deputy chairman of the Liberal Central Association said he had been told there were signs that seven or eight other local Conservative parties might withdraw candidates 'in order to get the Socialists out'. In the event these expectations were disappointed. In Middlesborough the Conservatives refused to allow Philip Fothergill a clear run in the West division; in Halifax negotiations for a 'Huddersfield formula' broke down; while in Dundee a different type of arrangement with the Conservatives met with little more success. Mr John Junor had been adopted as Liberal candidate for West Dundee, where his opponent would have been John Strachey. In February Mr Junor withdrew from the election, leaving Strachey to fight the Conservative candidate. A written agreement provided that the Dundee Liberals would not put up a candidate either in West Dundee or in East Dundee during the 1950 election, but at the next election the Conservatives would stand down in whichever constituency they failed to win. The Scottish Liberal Federation refused to endorse the agreement. It nominated its own candidate, whom the local Liberal Association refused to support. He was not successful at the election. Nor was Mr Junor at the 1951 contest in the same constituency, which the Conservatives did not fight. (To this limited extent, perhaps, the agreement can be described as a success.)[39] Between 1950 and 1951 attempts were made to extend the 'Huddersfield formula', but only in Bolton were the results a success. The situation was summarized by

[38] Nicholas, op. cit. pp. 82-3.
[39] ibid., pp. 83, 99, 255-6.

Churchill at Leeds on 4 February 1950. 'Here and there', he said, 'a sensible arrangement may be made but in the main the die is cast.'[40]

Would a Conservative-Liberal arrangement have been possible? Certainly the party was now further to the right than in 1945. A statement in the Liberal Candidates' Handbook went as follows: 'Every time the State takes taxes from the individual in his capacity as an income earner and pays it back in cash or kind in his capacity as a consumer or beneficiary under a State scheme (whether of direct subsidy or the subsidization of housing, education, medical benefit, social security or anything else) it reduces both the incentive to work and the apparent need to work.'[41] This was perhaps more reminiscent of Mr Martell (or, if one prefers it, Mr Enoch Powell) than of Lord Beveridge.

Nevertheless, the degree to which the party had moved to the right should not be exaggerated. In the period 1950-51 it was somehow suggested that, by opposing the nationalization of steel in Parliament, the Liberals were therefore turning decisively in the direction of the Conservatives. This is hardly fair. The Liberal record on steel was at least as consistent as that of any other party. At this time, the party summarized its objections to the Iron and Steel Bill as follows: First, there had been no impartial inquiry. Second, no thought had been given to the relationship of the nationalized companies with the Iron and Steel Corporation. Third, the powers and duties of the Minister were left vague: 'it is not, in our view, proper for any Minister to have a free hand to direct a basic industry through a corporation which would become the mere servant of the Minister.' And, fourth, the method of compensation was criticized.[42]

Apart from opposing steel nationalization, the Liberal Party urged thrift on the part of the Government. In the 1950 manifesto *No Easy Way* co-partnership and co-ownership were praised, free trade underplayed, peacetime conscription opposed and proportional representation proposed. There were to be family allowances for the first child. All ministerial orders were to be liable to challenge in the courts, no one was to be tried except in a court

[40] Quoted ibid. p. 92.

[41] Unattributed but quoted with approval, *Liberal Candidates' Handbook 1950*, p. 31.

[42] ibid. pp. 107-8.

of law and the powers of government inspectors to enter private premises was to be drastically reduced. A royal commission on the trade unions was to be set up: in the meanwhile contracting-in was to be substituted for contracting-out.

The manifesto promised that the Liberals would press for quicker action in developing the Council of Europe. European currencies should be convertible with one another: there was 'a joint responsibility to preserve democracy in Western Europe'.[43] Liberals such as Lord Layton and Lady Violet Bonham Carter had been among the first members of the united Europe movement. In May 1948 a large number of Liberals had attended the Congress of Europe at The Hague. In September of the same year the party had given support to the French proposal for a European Assembly. 'The Council of the Liberal Party,' went a resolution, 'realizing the urgent need for a political and economic union in Europe, welcomes the prompt action taken by France in supporting the proposal for the convening of a European consultative Assembly.' The resolution went on to call upon the Government, 'to give the plan their whole-hearted and immediate support'. The Government, of course, did nothing of the kind.

Europe apart, the most distinctive items of Liberal policy concerned co-ownership and free trade. Under the co-ownership plans there would be legislation requiring every industrial concern with a capital of more than £50,000, or more than fifty employees, to submit to a commission a scheme based on certain defined principles.[44] On free trade, the classic doctrine was laid down by Sir Andrew McFadyean. 'Liberals,' he wrote, 'stand alone in demanding free trade, and the next Liberal Government should restore it as our national economic policy. Liberals object to protection not merely as wrong in the circumstances of today. They believe that it destroys enterprise, restricts the consumer's freedom of choice, is a reprehensible method of invisible taxation, and is a fertile source of international friction.'[45] However, it would be wrong to imagine that free trade was emphasized by the Liberals. It was not. Indeed, at the pre-election emergency assembly of the party, some speakers objected to the resolution

[43] *No Easy Way* (Liberal Party, 1950), p. 8.

[44] For details of these principles, see *Liberal Candidates Handbook, 1950*, p. 96.

[45] Sir A. McFadyean, *The Liberal Case* (1950), p. 33.

pledging assured markets and guaranteed prices for farmers. Instead they wanted free trade. The resolution was however carried.[46]

The 1950 election will be remembered as the one in which the Liberals put up 475 candidates.[47] The basic decision to fight on as broad a front as possible had been taken by the whole party in April 1948. A year later, in his presidential address to the Hastings assembly, Sir Andrew McFadyean said that if a general election came 'tomorrow' the Liberals could put 300 candidates in the field. The object was to have 600 candidates ready to fight.[48] Of the 475 Liberals who did stand, those at West Huddersfield, Carmarthen, Greenock and the Western Isles were allowed a clear run by the Conservatives. Every one of the London boroughs and suburban constituencies were contested; and there was similarly impressive coverage in the North and East Ridings, in the Border country and the Highlands and Islands.[49]

The Liberals based their appeal in this election on their 'classlessness' and on the fact that they had put forward enough candidates to secure a majority in the House of Commons. 'If you want a Liberal Government you can have a Liberal Government'—this was the message Clement Davies gave in a party political film screened in cinemas throughout the country.[50] Other slogans included 'The Liberals can win' and 'At last you can have a Liberal Government'. Labour's reaction throughout the election was to ignore the Liberals. For example, in a broadcast on 4 February 1950 Herbert Morrison insisted that the real contest was between Conservative and Labour. The most the Liberals could hope to do would be to hold the balance. This was the only reference to the Liberals in Labour broadcasts. The Labour strategy was to pretend that the Liberals did not exist. The Conservatives, on the other hand, went out of their way to solicit Liberal votes. Churchill in particular emphasized this approach in his election

[46] *The Times*, 28 January 1950.

[47] When nominations closed on 13 February 1950, Lord Moynihan and Mr Edward Martell announced that over 470 candidates would be standing. The actual figure was 475, but owing to errors figures of 472 and 474 were released. On nomination day the *News Chronicle* ran a story headlined 'Liberals Keep Pledge, 472 to Fight'. Nicholas, op. cit. pp. 99, 162.

[48] *The Times*, 25 March 1949.

[49] Nicholas, op. cit. p. 42.

[50] At this time, of course, the cinema was more important as a means of communication than it is today.

address: he wrote of 'men like Morley, Grey and Asquith, whom I knew so well in my youth . . . individual liberty and State domination'.[51]

The Liberals, for their part, found it difficult to make very much impact. One reason was that they were perhaps rather ungenerously treated by the broadcasting authorities. Another was that they lacked names which made 'news'; or, rather, that the names which did make news were unable to give their whole time to national campaigning. Sir Archibald Sinclair, Clement Davies, Lady Megan Lloyd-George and Mr Frank Byers spent most of their time in their constituencies. Lady Violet Bonham Carter, it is true, did some touring: but she devoted most of her energies to the North. Generally the burden and heat of the day was borne by the peers, notably Lord Beveridge, Lord Samuel and Lord Milverton.

But their efforts were in vain. With 475 candidates, the party won only nine seats and lost 315 deposits. The most unfortunate casualty was probably Mr Byers, the Chief Whip, who lost North Dorset by ninety-seven votes. In only twenty-four seats did the party win a quarter of the vote or more, and all except three of these seats were in rural areas with a Liberal tradition. Though the total poll of 2,621,489 votes was an absolute advance on that of 1945 it was a relative decline. By no standards could the results be interpreted as good.[52]

Liberal Headquarters put as brave a face on the matter as it could. On the Saturday evening following the election a statement was issued which ran as follows: 'The Liberal Party carries on. Let there be no doubt about that. Backed by more than two and a half million people in all parts of the country, Liberals feel more than ever that in the end only Liberalism can solve the deadlock between the opposing Right and Left ideologies, which the election has thrown into such startling relief. Now that the party machines have crushed the independent, protection of the rights of minorities rests in the hands of Liberal Members of Parliament, and Liberals everywhere will back them to a man.' Similarly the *News Chronicle* declared that the Liberal performance would 'remain as a memorable and enduring protest against the insufferable tyranny of the sleek, soulless party machines that seek to dominate

[51] ibid. pp. 222-3.
[52] See ibid. pp. 299ff. and app. by D. E. Butler, p. 315.

the country'; and it criticized 'the insolence of those who would deny to Liberals the right to run their own candidates and the right to vote for their own party'. The *Manchester Guardian*, however, was more circumspect: though it defended the Liberals against the accusation that they had caused the narrow Labour victory of six seats, the *Guardian* thought it was 'a matter for deep discussion whether a thinly scattered vote of this kind can become the basis for a political party on national lines'; indeed the whole future of the Liberal Party might be at stake.

The *Daily Mail* blamed Liberal intervention for the Conservatives' narrow defeat, as did the *Daily Telegraph*, which went on to welcome 'the final and total eclipse of the Liberal Party' and to suggest that it ought to dissolve itself. *The Times* was if anything even more disapproving. A leader of 27 February 1950 declared that the controllers of the Liberal organization had performed 'a national disservice'. They had prevented the electorate from expressing its view on whether 'the policy of Socialism' was to be continued with. The article continued by deploring 'the irresponsible spattering of the electoral map with hundreds of candidates for which there never was the remotest chance of substantial support . . . it was never foreseen that a great and historic party would use its 'considerable [sic] financial resources to evade the spirit of the rule [on deposits]'.[53] The party could assist its cause 'by leaving, or helping, its supporters to judge for themelves which of the two larger parties can do most to put the Liberal spirit into practice'.[54]

How fair is it to say that the Liberals had 'let Labour in'? According to Dr Nicholas, if 30 per cent of the net Liberal vote had been transferred to the Conservatives they would have won seventeen Labour seats; a 20 per cent transfer would have produced twelve seats; a 10 per cent transfer, five.[55] Dr David Butler suggests[56] that in the rural areas there are to be found voters who will not vote for any pary but the Liberals. All in all, one can probably claim that if the number of Liberal candidates had been

[53] The party had paid a premium of £5,000 for which Lloyds underwrote all deposits lost after the first fifty up to a total of 250. The cost to Lloyds was £25,000. Herbert Morrison commented that Lloyds had 'lost a lot of money. The gentlemen of the City really should be more careful about politics, because they are not too well informed.'

[54] On all this see ibid. pp. 290ff.

[55] ibid. pp. 301f.

[56] ibid. pp. 318f.

drastically reduced, the Conservatives would have just won the election: but this is only guesswork.

'I must guard myself carefully,' said Winston Churchill in the debate on the address, 'against any suggestion of uttering what are called blandishments to the nine representatives of the Liberal Party, most of whom we see in their places under the guidance so generously provided by the Principality of Wales.'[57] Churchill then went on to quote the *Times* leader[58] approvingly and to lament the absence of a working majority. He said that a stalemate or deadlock had undoubtedly been produced in the effective government of the country. There was the certainty of a prolonged electioneering atmosphere at a time when the situation was critical both at home and abroad. However, said Churchill, it had perhaps been too readily assumed that the nine Liberals would occupy a position of exceptional and undue influence.

Clement Davies, for his part, denied that the Liberals would use such influence as they had irresponsibly. The government of the country, said Davies, had to be carried on: the people had voted and made their choice, and it was the duty of all M.P.s 'to take upon ourselves the responsibility put upon us'. Certainly, he said, the holding of another general election immediately or within the next two or three months was 'unthinkable'.[59]

The critical issue was still steel, and this was discussed two days later on a Conservative-moved amendment. The Liberal position was put by Mr Roderic Bowen, somewhat apologetically and with numerous interruptions. Mr Bowen said that 'there can be no question, in view of the attitude which the Liberals had adopted in relation to the Iron and Steel Act, of their supporting the Government in regard to this Amendment. The difficulty which arises (interruptions) . . . is that we, in common with the Conservatives, regard the proposal to nationalize iron and steel as a vital one—as the Socialists do for different reasons. It is vital because it will have very grave consequences upon the national economy and the welfare of the country as a whole. In those circumstances, much as we regret that this question should be raised on this occasion, we feel that, in view of the strong and consistent attitude we have always adopted throughout in this matter, it is necessary for us to

[57] 472 H.C. Deb. 5s., 141 (7 March 1950).
[58] See above.
[59] ibid. 157.

support this Amendment (i.e. vote with the Conservatives)'.[60] It may be noted that Lady Megan Lloyd George, a persistent critic of any tendencies to be over-friendly towards the Right, on this occasion voted with her party and with the Conservatives.

Shortly afterwards two Liberal peers, Lord Reading and Lord Rennell of Rodd, decided to transfer their support to the Conservative Party, which they regarded as 'the only party capable of offering effective resistance to Socialism'.[61] They were followed into the Conservative Party by another brace of peers, Lord Willingdon and the wealthy Lord Cowdray.[62] More important than these defections, however, was a speech by Lord Woolton in which he said that a widespread demand existed for the unity of those opposed to Socialism. He said that the political prejudices of parties or individuals must not be allowed to stand in the way of united action when parties with different names were agreed on basic principles. These 'principles' included opposition to any increased powers of the State, to nationalization and to centralization. But Liberals and Conservatives were united in support of partnership in industry, high employment, a prosperous economy, a healthy nation, adequate defences and tolerance.[63] Lord Woolton might just as well have added, for good measure, that Liberals and Conservatives were united in support of virtue and in opposition to vice. Nevertheless, what his 'nine-point plan' lacked in precision it made up for in political impact. At least it led to a three-hour meeting of the Liberal Party Committee, at the conclusion of which Clement Davies issued this statement: 'The Liberal Party Committee assures Liberals in the country that it has no intention of compromising the independence of the Liberal Party.'[64]

But Churchill, who had approved Woolton's proposal, did not entirely give up hope. Though he denied that any negotiations were going on between Liberals and Conservatives, he said that he would still like to see an 'honourable understanding' reached with the Liberal Party. If that were not possible an understanding might be reached with individual Liberals. It was a moment, declared Churchill, when 'we have the right to appeal to all patriotic and broadminded men and women who are in agreement on the main issues to do their utmost to secure the establishment of a

[60] ibid. 500 (9 March 1950).
[61] *The Times*, 15 April 1950.
[62] ibid. 5 May 1950.
[63] ibid. 1 May 1950.
[64] ibid. 3 May 1950.

strong, broadly based and stable Government capable of dealing in a courageous and progressive spirit with the ever-darkening problems that confront us.'[65]

At the Party's Scarborough Assembly Mr Byers, the chairman of the Executive, confirmed Churchill's denial of any negotiations; but Lady Megan retained her suspicions; though she did not directly accuse the leadership of parleying with the enemy, she emphasized that there had been a 'shift to the right'. A certain amount of evidence in her favour was provided by events in Bolton and Colne Valley. In Bolton the terms under which the local Conservative and Liberal parties agreed to fight the election laid down that the Liberal candidate would 'at all times fight against any measures of nationalization . . . and for the repeal of the Iron and Steel Nationalization Act'. Whereas in Colne Valley the local Conservative Association offered to support Lady Violet Bonham Carter if she became Liberal candidate. The Bolton arrangement, at least, was in contravention of Liberal policy on straight fights, as laid down by the party council in March 1951 (though oddly enough this policy was stated to apply only to by-elections). The Liberal Party, declared the council, was completely free and independent. It had no pact, agreement or understanding with any other party. It would maintain, both in and out of Parliament, completely unfettered independence to advocate the distinctive Liberal policy and programme. Therefore no action should be taken, either at national or at local level, to place a candidate under any obligation—express or implied, open or secret—to act, speak or vote otherwise than in accordance with Liberal principles and his own judgement and conscience.

The tempters had on the whole been successfully resisted.

[65] Speech at Edinburgh, ibid. 20 May 1950.

CHAPTER IV

THE DARKEST DAYS

In the general election of 1951 the Liberal Party lost three seats. Its parliamentary representation was reduced to six. It polled 722,679 votes, compared to 2,621,489 in the previous election. It had put only 109 candidates into the contest. The election, and the period which followed it, was, as Philip Fothergill was later to remark, the lowest point ever in the party's fortunes.

For a view of the party's condition at this time it is worth turning to Mr Edward Martell. Mr Martell, though regarded with considerable suspicion by members of the Liberal hierarchy, was in a good position to know what was wrong. This does not mean that he was disinterested; then, as now, Mr Martell was a man of strong and idiosyncratic opinions. But he had met with great success as a Liberal fund raiser; he had been more than anyone else responsible for the fielding of 475 candidates in 1950; he had been close to the party's leadership, yet never entirely of it. On 31 October 1951 Mr Martell addressed a twelve-page memorandum to 'the Leaders of the Liberal Party'. In it he put forward four reasons for the party's catastrophic performance in the election. First, wrote Mr Martell, no national plan of campaign was put into operation between the election of 1950 and that of 1951. Second, the party had fought twenty-nine seats where it had lost deposits in 1950; had not fought thirty-four good seats; and had made little or no attempt to place the best candidates in the best seats. Third, Liberal waverers had been confused by the emphasis put by some Liberal leaders—particularly Lady Violet Bonham Carter—on getting the Socialists out rather than the Liberals in. Fourth, wrote Mr Martell, warming to his theme on Lady Violet, her 'blatant pro-Tory attitude dismayed many in the Party who had hitherto held her in the highest respect, and destroyed the public belief in our independence. After all, she holds high office in the party'.

'In short,' concluded Mr Martell, 'we could not have gone into a general election in a more haphazard or rudderless way . . . Our present sorry plight is almost entirely due to lack of leadership and every one of the officers is in some part responsible. If only one of them had insisted on the position being faced, or had resigned in protest and told the Council and Executive why, it would have been possible to enter the election with some chance of at least maintaining our position. As it was we never stood a chance from the beginning. It cannot be said that no warning was given, for my Memo of 13 March 1951 . . . fortold exactly what would happen if nothing was done.'

This previous memorandum set out, under a wealth of numbered sub-headings (for which Mr Martell has a passion), the defects in the Liberal Party. Altogether, according to Mr Martell, there were thirteen of them.[1] But the basis of his criticism was that the Liberal Party was in a condition of visible disintegration, and that nothing was being done to reverse the process.

After the election of 1951, Mr Martell considered that his gloomy prognostications had been amply justified. But he was not yet ready to wash his hands of the party. All was not lost. Mr Martell proposed that an emergency assembly should be called in November or early December. At this gathering the party constitution should be amended. In virtue of this amendment, area federations would be abolished and replaced by smaller groups of constituency associations. The autonomy of associations would be restricted. All party officers and committee members, at every level, would be bound to accept the decisions of the committee on which they served. The votes of the Assembly and of the Liberal Party Council would be by ballot and not by show of hands. Finally, party membership would be by card only.

The election which had just ended certainly gave some support to Mr Martell's despondent analysis. In Anglesey Lady Megan Lloyd George lost her seat after twenty-two years' service as Member for the constituency. In Colne Valley Lady Violet Bonham Carter failed yet again in her effort to enter the House of Commons, even though no Conservative candidate stood against her and Sir Winston Churchill journeyed to Huddersfield to speak on her behalf. It is arguable, of course, that the Liberal Party in Parliament was more harmonious for the absence of these two

[1] General political position; general state of the party; public view; general strategy; election prospects; election plans; straight fight arrangements; leadership; finance; parliamentary unity, the *Liberal News*; candidates; and discipline.

from its ranks; for Lady Megan was moving rapidly to the Left, Lady Violet just as rapidly to the Right. But despite their predilection for quarrelling—partly, perhaps, because of it—they were undoubtedly the best-publicised members of the Liberal Party. And, at a period when the Liberal Party received little publicity, their absence from Parliament could hardly be anything other than a blow.

Nor were they the only losses. Mr Emrys Roberts was defeated at Merioneth, a Liberal stronghold for over 50 years. Mr A. J. F. Macdonald and Mr Edgar Granville both lost their seats. Apart from Mr Jo Grimond (who was returned at Orkney and Shetland) only those Liberals who were not opposed by Conservatives retained their seats. They were Mr Clement Davies, Mr Roderic Bowen, Mr R. Hopkin Morris and Mr Donald Wade. Of those Liberals who had not been in the previous Parliament, and were not opposed by Conservatives, the only successful one was Mr Arthur Holt at West Bolton; the other two—Lady Violet at Colne Valley and Mr John Junor at West Dundee—both failed to win.

Looking back, it was all inevitable. It was as apparent to the electors as to the politicians that the Liberals were entering this election a depleted and leaderless army. Of course the Liberal manifesto put on as brave a face as it could. The existence of the party, said the manifesto, constantly reminded the individual M.P. that 'the crack of the party whip' was 'by no means the be-all and end-all of a Live Democracy'.[2] That (the manifesto went on) was why Liberals were convinced that there should be more of their members in the House of Commons. In an effort to bring this about, the party would 'contest selected seats in all areas of the country, and concentrate all their resources on those constituencies'. In so doing, said the manifesto, the Liberals offered to the nation 'an opportunity of sending to Parliament first-class men and women who have a great contribution to make to the solution of our problems; men and women who will fight without fear for the policies they think best for the nation, whether they are popular policies or not'.[3]

Whether Liberal policies were popular or not, they were certainly not very clear. The manifesto proposed a 'great national

[2] *The Nation's Task* (1951).
[3] ibid.

drive' to decrease prices. In contrast to the policy of 1950, food subsidies were to remain until the increased productivity campaign had brought down the cost of living. The Council of Europe was to be supported. Prosperity was to be stimulated by encouragements to invest in new plant. Monopolies were to be attacked, building costs to be cut. There would be guaranteed prices for agriculture, and parliaments for Scotland and Wales. It was not the most exciting of programmes.

Nor was the manifesto at all convincing when it claimed that the Liberals were contesting 'selected' seats. It was a curious process of selection which decreed that the Liberals should not fight Torrington, Caernarvon, and Kinross and West Perthshire—all constituencies where their candidate had been runner-up in 1950. The truth was, of course, that there was hardly any conscious selection of seats. The Liberal Party was the prisoner of events. At the beginning of the campaign the party had 174 candidates. Many of them then withdrew 'for business reasons'; and some constituencies discovered that they did not have enough money to fight.[4] Naturally enough, the predominant note struck was one of self-justification rather than self-confidence.

From the Liberal point of view, the most striking event immediately following the election was the offer of a Cabinet post to Clement Davies. There seems little doubt that Churchill made this offer less from calculation than from a genuine feeling of goodwill towards the Liberal Party. Churchill, almost alone among leading post-war Conservatives, treated the Liberals with respect, despite his criticism that they ought really to join his own party. Besides, the Conservative majority in the House of Commons was seventeen: it was perfectly workable without Liberal support. On 28 Ocober 1951, however, Churchill and Davies met at Chartwell. Later Davies had talks with leading Liberals. He then made public his refusal to join the Churchill Administration, 'The Liberal Party,' went a subsequent statement, 'is deeply concerned at the possible effect of the narrow majority in the House of Commons . . . upon the successful conduct of policy both in domestic and in international affairs. In these circumstances it will both in Parliament and in the country give to the Government support for measures clearly conceived in the interest of the country as a whole.' Davies echoed this at a luncheon at the National Liberal

[4] See D. E. Butler, *The British General Election of 1951* (1952), p. 95.

Club. He pledged his party to support the Government, not because it was Conservative, but because it was 'charged with the heavy responsibility of guiding the nation through the rapids into more peaceful waters'. The Liberals would support the Conservatives so long as the measures taken by them were in the best interests of the country as a whole, and not a particular section.[5]

Support for the Conservatives, however, was hardly calculated to satisfy even the most watery Liberal. Something had clearly to be done; and there were many suggestions put forward about what this should be. Mr Deryck Abel, for instance, advanced an ambitious scheme[6] which comprised:

(i) An overall strategy 'applying lessons from the four-stage Labour Party strategy of 1906-51'.

(ii) A tactical plan of concentration on, say, five or six classes of constituencies, with strictly equal treatment for each; these constituencies would then form a 'bridge-head' for a 'general assault'.

(iii) A five-year publicity and psychological warfare programme to build up twenty-five to forty national names in addition to the existing nine or ten.

(iv) A campaign in political education to show the difference between the Liberals and the other two parties.

(v) 'The creation of a new school of philosophic thought, which will carry on the work of the Benthamite Philosophic Radicals of the early nineteenth century.'

(vi) An avoidance of phrasing in questionnaires which enabled opposition candidates to shirk direct issues.

(vii) No appearances by Liberals on Conservative or Labour platforms.

(viii) Constant exposure of and comment on injustices.

More significant than Mr Abel's somewhat quaintly-assorted proposals were those of seventeen other Liberals, including Mr Martell. Most of these seventeen had been candidates at the previous election, and three were members of the Liberal Executive. In a letter to the *Liberal News* of 27 November 1951, they said that 'the pathetic rabble we have been for so long can never achieve anything'. The first duty of the party, they wrote, was

[5] *The Times*, 22 November 1951.
[6] Letter in *News Chronicle*, 3 December 1951-.

'to agree upon some measure of discipline . . . The case . . . seems to us to be unanswerable. If we band ourselves together as a political party it can only be in order to work together to achieve common aims. If we claim, in the name of liberty, the right to work and speak in public against each other we are no longer a party and we can never achieve anything.' The letter put forward several proposals calculated to increase party discipline. First, membership of the party should be by card only. Second, all officers and committee members at all levels of the party should be bound to accept and support in public majority decisions of the committees on which they served. Third, the local autonomy of constituency associations should be limited so that they could not (for example) fight a seat if to do so would be against Liberal strategy. And, fourth, Parliamentary candidates should be bound to support official policy in public.

These proposals were rejected at a private Liberal convention held at the Kingsway Hall, though it was reported that 'there is greater backing in the party for the idea of selected candidatures than the decision of the convention might suggest . . . A number of Liberals doubt whether the party can benefit in any way when candidates are run without a chance of success and with a fair chance of forfeiting their deposits'.[7] What the convention did decide was that the party should fight on 'the widest possible front'. Constituencies were to be encouraged to form new associations and to strengthen existing ones. But priority was to be given to those constituencies where the Liberal poll was good in the 1950 and 1951 elections. The convention also decided something else: to appoint a paid director-general who would take charge of the party organization throughout the country.

This was something more than a purely organizational decision. It demonstrated the determination of the party to fight on. And here some tribute should perhaps be paid to those Liberals who, in the dark days of 1951 and 1952, kept the faith: Philip Fothergill, Clement Davies, Mr Frank Byers and others. It would have been easy for any of these to find a satisfactory, perhaps a glorious,

[7] *Guardian*, 17 December 1951. The Liberals held this convention because the leaders wanted an early meeting representative of the whole party. They were advised that plans for a party assembly (which would have had the authority to instruct the executive) could not be completed in time. Hence this convention, which met in private because its decisions were advisory only.

future with one or other of the major parties. Davies, as we have seen, could have had a post in the Churchill Cabinet. Yet he stood firm. 'There is work for all hands,' he said—employing one of those nautical metaphors which came so easily to him—'on the Liberal ship.'[8] 'We refuse to be stamped out,' he said to the Liberal Assembly. 'In spite of all temptations we still prefer our own doctrine and we are determined to maintain our independence.'[9] Mr Byers took the same line both with the Assembly and in an appeal for funds to promote electoral reform.[10] Mr Byers, however, went further than his leader. So far as one can tell, he was the first Liberal, apart from Sir Roy Harrod,[11] to urge the formation of that radical non-Socialist party which was later to be proposed by Mr Grimond. Such a party, said Mr Byers, would provide 'the right government for this country. The Opposition would consist on the right of the Blimps, and on the left of the Bevanites. That sort of government would give us a chance to re-establish Britain as a force in international affairs'.[12]

This prospect had little appeal for Lady Violet Bonham Carter, at least as far as the immediate present was concerned. She suggested that Liberals should get together and decide to cast a 'solid and united' vote which would determine the result of the general election. They should cast it for the party which would pledge itself to Liberal policies and would be prepared to 'face the facts' and 'do its duty to the nation'. Clearly Lady Violet did not have the Labour Party in mind. 'Which one of us,' she inquired, 'can be a neutral at this moment? Is there one of us, whatever our ideology, who would be prepared to entrust our economic policy, our foreign policy or our defence policy to the Socialist Party in its present state of civil war?'[13] Lady Violet had previously had a little trouble over standing at Colne Valley. The Bethnal Green Association asked the Liberal Executive to call for her resignation. They claimed that by contesting the seat with Conservative support she 'stabbed every Liberal candidate in the back'. Mr Byers, the chairman of the Executive, said that the request was 'most

[8] New Year message, *The Times*, January 1952.
[9] *The Times*, 19 May 1952.
[10] The appeal was also signed by Philip Fothergill and Major General W. H. Grey.
[11] See above, ch. III, p. 43.
[12] Speech at Kensington, *News Chronicle*, 4 November 1952.
[13] Speech at Manchester, *The Times*, 3 April 1952.

unlikely to be regarded with any favour whatsoever', for the party was against 'heresy hunts and post-mortems of this kind'. Subsequently Lady Violet turned down an invitation to fight Colne Valley at the forthcoming election, on the ground that nursing the constituency would interfere with the rest of her public work.[14] The Liberal Party Council subsequently administered an implicit rebuke to Lady Violet. A resolution passed by the Council asserted again the determination of the party to continue as an independent political force; and it stated that in no circumstances would the Liberals fight in union with any other political party 'on the negative one-point policy of anti-nationalization'.[15]

The Liberal Party, then, was to be independent. But what precisely did this mean? Clearly independence did not exclude local arrangements on the Huddersfield pattern. Nor, maintained the Liberal commentator A. J. Cummings, should the party be reluctant to use its strength in the marginal constituencies. The voting figures at the previous election, wrote Cummings, showed that in about forty seats the Liberals held a clear balance of power. In all these constituencies Liberals should make use of their strength. They could put pressure on both Labour and the Conservatives.[16] The Liberal Party, he wrote, 'must puff away the little Bethel atmosphere of exclusiveness which had been confused with political independence and must take early and united action in the constituencies'.[17] Cummings did not specify the conditions under which such intervention should take place; nor was he clear about its exact purpose. Yet his words were not entirely in vain. The Executive of the party decided to fight, not only those seats where a Liberal candidate had a reasonable chance of winning, but also the marginal seats where intervention might prove decisive to Conservative or Labour chances. The party, the Executive made clear, would not concentrate its main effort in those marginal constituencies. It would add them to the list of areas where a Liberal would be encouraged to come forward. This strategy, it was pointed out, was not being adopted with a view to securing electoral parts. Its object was to bring influence to bear

[14] See *Daily Express*, 4 and 5 January and 18 September 1952.
[15] *The Times*, 15 December 1952.
[16] *News Chronicle*, 27 May 1952.
[17] ibid. 6 June 1952.

upon the policies of both the other parties by demonstrating Liberal strength.

But this strategy, indeed no strategy of any kind, could be effective without an improvement in party organization. Mr Byers had the matter in hand. He conceived the idea of 'Operation Basic', a kind of Doomsday survey of local parties. The operation was begun in January 1952. Teams from party headquarters led by Philip Fothergill (the party president) and Mr Byers worked out with local officials plans to increase membership and reorganize finances. The first stage was to compile a full record of membership and finances of each local party. A target for increase in membership was then agreed upon: in some constituencies it was hoped to grow by 50 per cent within six months. As far as finance was concerned, the general aim was to enable constituencies, or groups of constituencies, to engage a paid organizer at around £450 a year. The *Guardian* described one such foray: 'The plan followed during the week-end is to be applied generally throughout the inquiries. Mrs Gorsky and her team arrived in Bristol on Friday and met the officials of six constituency associations. On Saturday she went to Trowbridge to see the officials of four more constituencies; Mr Byers saw other officials in Trowbridge in the morning, and in the afternoon the two teams joined with representatives of the Western and Bristol constituencies for a general meeting.'[18]

But what, in the end, was the purpose of these comings and goings? What did the Liberals want to see done? They wanted, for one thing, a Liberties of the Subject Act. In the House of Lords, on 16 July 1952, Lord Samuel, the leader of the Liberal peers, moved a resolution on the liberties of the subject. It called for legislation to give effect to the proposals of the Bill which he had introduced in 1950. The Bill proposed to provide more effective parliamentary control over statutory instruments and over the nationalized boards. It wanted all the recommendations of the 1932 Committee on Ministers' Powers to be put into effect. There was to be a restriction of the authority given to departmental officials to enter and search private premises. The defendant in an agricultural marketing board case was to have the option of being heard by a court of law. The distinction between public authorities and private individuals was to be abolished when limitation of

[18] *Guardian*, 31 March 1952.

actions was concerned. Lastly, it would be illegal for employers to impose any political, religious or racial test as a condition of employment. In 1950 the House of Lords had given the Bill a second reading by 66 votes to 24, though it was opposed by the Labour Government. Conservative peers who had voted in its favour included Lords Swinton, Woolton and Cherwell; while Lord Carrington had acted as one of the tellers. But the Conservatives, once in office, were less well-disposed towards the Bill. Lord Salisbury gave it little hope, and moved an amendment which Lord Samuel said he would not challenge. The resolution as amended read: 'That this House, considering that various encroachments upon the liberties of the subject have taken place in recent years, would favour the progressive restoration of such liberties as and when the national situation allows.' (The year, it should be remembered, was 1952!)[19] What was significant about Lord Samuel's Bill was not its concern for liberty—strong and sincere though this was—but the old-fashioned nature of the remedies it proposed. The homage paid to the Donoughmore Committee, the idea that Parliament could somehow legislate itself into greater authority, the demand that the courts should be the guarantors of freedom for agriculturalists—all this had little connection with reality. It belonged to another age.[20]

And many Liberals, while not being opposed to Lord Samuel or to his views on liberty, were concerned at the influence which the followers of Adam Smith still possessed in the party. The Radical Reform Group was formed to counteract this influence. It was, in essence, a group of Keynesians who also claimed an affinity with Asquith and Beveridge. In a statement of principle, the Radical Reformers said they had long believed that a third force in British politics should find its inspiration in the Liberal synthesis of freedom and social reform. They felt sure, they wrote, that many besides themselves had been alarmed at two trends which had been apparent in the Liberal Party in previous months. First, there had been a tendency to attack the whole conception

[19] See Lord Samuel, *The People's Liberties* (Liberal Party, 1952).

[20] This is not the place to go into the questions of parliamentary supremacy, delegated legislation and administrative law raised by Lord Samuel's motion. However, it may be noted that the judges have shown themselves reluctant to assume powers *vis-a-vis* actions by authorities such as marketing boards; and that, when they have done so, there has been little sign of any bias in favour of the citizen.

of the Welfare State, the foundations of which had been laid by the Liberal Government of 1906. And, second, a section within the party had been loud in its advocacy of an economic doctrine which was pure *laissez-faire*. 'We strongly deplore both these tendencies,' wrote the reformers, 'and believe that the majority of active Liberals would agree with us. We have, therefore, formed the Radical Reform Group with the object of promoting, within the Liberal Party, the policy of social reform without Socialism which Liberals have developed from 1908 onwards.' The signatories were Messrs. A. J. F. Macdonald, E. F. Allison, Desmond Banks, Norman Clarke, Peter Grafton and Philip Skelsey.[21] It is worth noting that this group, though against *laissez-faire*, were in favour of free (or at least very much freer) trade—a cause which won considerable support at the Ilfracombe Assembly of the party and was the subject of a pamphlet[22] by Mr Deryck Abel, a member of the Liberal Executive. Indeed Cross-bencher of the *Sunday Express* considered the Liberal free traders such a menace that he offered to finance candidates who would fight against them in the Liberals' three Welsh seats.[23] But the prospective candidates who presented themselves were not inspiring, and the project was quickly abandoned.

It is difficult to estimate with any precision the influence which the Radical Reform Group exercised within the party. It is possible to see the group as a precursor of the revolution which was later to be put into effect by Mr Grimond. Certainly many of the young men in the universities were either Radical Reformers or sympathetic to the movement's aims. In Cambridge, particularly, the generation of Mr Richard Moore, Mr Derick Mirfin and Dr Timothy Joyce were ahead of their time. They were tired of the old men of the party. They were looking forward to Mr Grimond three years before he in fact arrived. For the Liberal Party remained inclined towards the Right. The existence of the Radical Reform Group showed as much. If the situation had been otherwise the group would not have been set up in the first place. And this inclination to the Right was also responsible for many of the defections which occurred in this period. For instance, Mr Edgar Granville, who had sat as Liberal M.P. for Eye until his defeat in

[21] Letter in *Guardian*, 27 March 1953.
[22] *Free Trade Challenge* (Liberal Publications, 1953).
[23] *Sunday Express*, 14 June 1953.

1951, joined the Labour Party. Mr Dingle Foot withdrew as prospective candidate for North Cornwall; and, though he remained in the party until after the 1955 election, it was widely believed that he was planning to leave. Moreover, there were other, less widely-publicised defections: for example, the President of the Birmingham Women's Liberal Association left the party to join Labour. The cumulative effect of these desertions was highly depressing for the party; the more so since they were combined with the loss of Mr Byers as candidate for North Dorset and of Mrs Gorsky as candidate for Carlisle. Mr Byers resigned both because of his business activities and because of his national work for the party; Mrs Gorsky because of her appointment as editor of a women's television programme.

But though the Liberals had lost Mr Granville, and were in the process of losing Mr Foot, they had gained Mr Herbert Harris. The private convention of December 1951, it will be remembered, decided that a director-general of the party should be appointed. For months and months the search went on. No one suitable could be found. Though the salary for the post was at least £2,500, Mr Byers said—presumably he was making a joke—that he would be prepared to pay the right man £8,500.[24] Furthermore, the conditions of work, as set out by Mr Byers, were highly congenial: 'he could just sit and think for as long as he wanted,' said Mr Byers, 'provided he brings in the results.'[25] Still no one suitable turned up. Finally someone did. Mr Harris came to the party after a career with Pitman's Colleges, and was paid the markedly high salary, for a political organizer, of £3,500 a year. Fifteen months had passed since the original decision had been made at the Kingsway Hall. Mr Harris, however, started to think at once; and his conclusions were sombre. 'We find ourselves,' he said in a letter to Liberal Federation secretaries, 'in such parlous straits that we have enough funds to sustain ourselves, at the most, only to the end of September, with little chance of further moneys accruing.'[26] But in fact Mr Harris was being unnecessarily gloomy. Somehow the good ship Liberal—as Clement Davies might well have put it—kept afloat. For one thing, the party was helped by the length of the 1951-5 Parliament: an election in late 1953 or early 1954 would have meant a very different story. For another, Liberalism

[24] *Daily Express*, 6 May 1952. [25] ibid.
[26] ibid. 20 June 1953.

was still interesting and exciting, at least for its adherents. The conflicts which were carried on within the party were not, of course, comparable (either in intensity or in the publicity they received) to the conflicts inside the Labour Party: but they were real conflicts all the same. The party assembly of April 1954 was enlivened by the threat of the Radical Reform Group to boycott a motion on party unity, though at the last moment the Group withdrew its opposition. At a press conference which preceded the assembly Philip Fothergill, the chairman of the Executive, and Sir Andrew McFadyean discounted suggestions of party disunity. The Executive, said Fothergill, was 'certainly not hostile' to the Group. On the contrary, it took 'an extremely tolerant view of people in any part of the party who got down to the job of research and policy production.' Sir Andrew pointed to a resolution on unity of purpose, to be moved by Mr Mirfin of Cambridge on behalf of the Union of University Liberal Societies, and seconded by Mr Geoffrey Acland on behalf of the Executive. The resolution recognized 'that there are, and always have been, two distinct and interdependent traditions in Liberal thought, but believes that the task of the Liberal Party today is to blend these two traditions in a unified policy of social justice and economic strength'.[27]

But whom were the Radical Reformers really against? Were they against the old men (and old women) of the party? Or were they against the doctrinaire free traders and opponents of the Welfare State such as Mr S. W. Alexander and Major Oliver Smedley? It was the latter group which had laid the foundations for the free trade success at the Ilfracombe Assembly[28] and certainly its views were extreme. 'I say, and shall continue to say,' declared Major Smedley, 'that the worst thing you can do with your money is to hand it over to be spent by the State . . . Far better keep it in your money-box and sleep with it under your pillow at night. But, better still, invest it in your business or someone else's business. Anywhere is better than letting it pass through the slippery fingers of the State. *There is no need yet for a campaign for the non-payment of taxes, lawfully levied and assessed.* But the handing-over of our savings to the State is not yet compulsory, and there we have an opportunity of making our pro-

[27] *Guardian*, 1 April 1954.
[28] See R. Pitman in *Tribune*, 17 April 1953.

test against Government extravagance. Money is losing value because the Government will not exercise control over their own expenditure and the constantly-expanding issue of paper money with which they finance it.'[29]

Views of this kind were not, of course, typical of any but a small group inside the party (though it is noteworthy that Major Smedley was still a member of the Executive when he made this speech. Furthermore, the Executive, as far as one can gather, administered no reproof.) A member of the Liberal Party Council, Mr Paul Rose, claimed that the members of the Radical Reform Group were under a misapprehension. The views of Major Smedley and Mr Alexander, wrote Mr Rose, were being identified by Radical Reformers with the views of those Liberals who believed in a free economy. Mr Banks and his colleagues (he went on) should be aware that the extreme free-traders had always differed from the belief, more widely-held by Liberals, that a free economy and a welfare society were really complementary necessities. It seemed as if the Group was unable to realize that all items of Liberal policy formed part of 'a comprehensive whole'.[30]

And yet, in this period of doubt and self-questioning, there was one ray of light. Just before Christmas 1954 the Liberals came second in the Inverness by-election. True, their candidate was the formidable John M. Bannerman, Rugby international and speaker of Gaelic; true, also, nothing very much could be deduced from an election in a constituency as far-flung as Inverness: but the result showed that there was still some vigour in the party. The figures were:

N. L. D. McLean (Conservative)	10,329
J. M. Bannerman (Liberal)	8,998
W. Paterson (Labour)	5,642
Conservative maj.	1,331

The result showed something else: that there was still some vigour in Clement Davies. Before the poll Sir Winston Churchill sent a message to the Conservative candidate in which he said that to vote Liberal would be to 'shirk' the issue. 'It looks to me,' replied

[29] Speech at Stratford-on-Avon, reported *Glasgow Herald*, 5 April 1955. *My italics.*

[30] Letter in *Guardian*, 23 April 1954.

the Liberal leader, 'as if the doctrine of Fascism has entered the doors of 10 Downing Street.'[31] And, in his New Year message, Davies returned to the offensive, talking about Sir Winston's 'cool effrontery' and about his being 'wrapped round with the patchwork robe of the Tory leader'.[32]

Meanwhile, Mr Herbert Harris had not been idle. In April 1954 he had announced that between 120 and 200 Liberal candidates would stand at the election. In 1955 he revealed that in 1954 party membership had gone up by 50 per cent. 'We shall fight the next general election,' he said, 'in a series of selected seats, and we are unrepentant in saying that we do this because of our limited resources. But we shall surprise both the Conservatives and the Socialists by the campaign we shall carry on in every constituency in the country.[33]

There was hope yet.

[31] *Daily Express*, 15 December 1954.
[32] *Guardian*, 31 December 1954.
[33] *News Chronicle*, 17 February 1955.

CHAPTER V

ENTER MR GRIMOND

THE general election campaign of 1955 did not find the Liberal Party in very happy circumstances. It was a divided party. On 26 April Lady Megan Lloyd George, to the accompaniment of much publicity, announced her conversion to Socialism, or, more strictly perhaps, to the Labour Party: for Lady Megan had always, and possibly at undue length, insisted that she was a 'Radical'. As she put it, 'in the changed situation of today it is only in the Labour Party that I can be true to the radical tradition'.[1] Naturally the defection was a distressing event, but it could not be helped. The warning signals had been emanating from Lady Megan for some time; and certainly Lady Violet Bonham Carter was not in the least surprised at the desertion. Radicals, as she explained to Lord Samuel two months later, were not to be trusted an inch. Writing to him when he retired from the Liberal leadership in the Lords, Lady Violet declared that 'whatever you call yourself, you will always lead . . . it is hard for those who remember the great men of our Party to continue to serve its shadow among the lesser ones. But while you remain—as you do—we are still linked with the tradition of greatness. . . . Joe Chamberlain became the mainspring of Protection and Imperialism; Lloyd George sold the Liberal Party to the Tories in 1918. Such things are possible for so-called Radicals—impossible for any Liberal—you—my father—Edward Grey'.[2]

Lady Megan was not the only trouble. Clement Davies, the Leader, was ill, and unable to attend the Llandudno Assembly of the party. The election was announced while the Assembly was in progress. Clearly some stirring words were necessary. But who was to deliver them? The man who stepped forward was Mr. Joseph Grimond (as he was then generally called). And Mr. Grimond exceeded all expectations. The Liberals, wrote Dr Butler, 'were sent back to their constituencies heartened by a rousing and

[1] Quoted D. E. Butler, *The British General Election of 1955* (1955), p. 69.
[2] Quoted J. Bowle, *Viscount Samuel* (1957), p. 357.

common-sense speech'[3] and the *Guardian* commented, in a passage which is worth quoting at length. 'The Chief Whip had not hitherto revealed himself very clearly to the party, although he had spoken in a modest, rather diffident way at previous assemblies—a reluctant hero if ever there was one. On Saturday he spoke with such firmness, breadth of view and authority that delegates rose to him as to a man capable of leadership in the future. When Mr Grimond had finished speaking he was warmly applauded. Then the delegates rose in their places and stood, clapping enthusiastically, for a minute or so. But the effect of the speech was more lasting than that. Delegates took away with them a new hope such as they have scarcely dared to expect since the war.'[4]

Yet, despite Mr. Grimond's best endeavours, it cannot be pretended that in the 1955 contest the Liberals made any great impact either on the electorate or on the tactics of the major parties. It was, in any event, a quiet campaign, the most quiet since the war; and the Liberals did nothing to enliven it. Their manifesto, published on 6 May, bore the somewhat forbidding title of *Crisis Unresolved*. This proposed a limitation on the use of the veto by the great powers at the United Nations. It advocated more British enthusiasm for European Union. It promised to attack monopolies and to set up a Royal Commission on the trade unions. It said that farm subsidies could be abolished if farmers' costs were lowered by removing tariffs on imports and attacking monopolies of farm equipment. Above all, the manifesto put forward the familiar thesis that the Liberal Party, being tied to no sectional interest, was more likely to do the patriotic and decent thing.[5] All in all, there was little here to set the blood coursing more powerfully through anyone's veins. As the political correspondent of the *Guardian* wrote, presumably putting the most favourable construction he could on it, 'the most distinctive features of the Liberal Party's election manifesto . . . are an appeal to the middle-class vote and an attack, in the name of liberty, on the tendency of trade unions to limit the freedom of individuals within the unions'.[6]

[3] Butler, *The British General Election of 1955*, p. 68.
[4] *Guardian*, 18 April 1955.
[5] cf. Leonard Behrens, President-elect of the Liberal Party Organisation, letter ibid. 22 April 1955.
[6] ibid. 6 May 1955.

And yet it would be wrong to put the blame for the Liberals' lack of impact on their manifesto. The climate of a general election is rarely influenced by the one or two thousand words put out by the parties shortly before the contest. Nor, it seems, does the campaign as a whole matter nearly so much as was once believed by the theorists of nineteenth century representative government. The election of 1955 was no exception. It fell into the political trough which formed between Korea and Suez. It was the end of the period of Butskellism. It did not appear to the voters to be about anything. Where the two main parties failed, the Liberals can hardly be blamed for failing also.

Furthermore, they put up only 110 candidates—one more than in 1951. There was little interest in whether they would 'split the vote' or 'let the Tories in'. Most of the major parties' effort was concentrated on winning Liberal votes in constituencies where no Liberal candidate was standing. The Labour Party exploited the defection of Lady Megan. The Conservatives emphasized their belief in freedom. Winston Churchill, ever more attentive to the Liberals than were the rest of his Cabinet colleagues, wrote in his election address that he hoped 'to carry with me my Liberal friends in Woodford, and perhaps elsewhere, in this election. There is a broad harmony between the aims of modern Tory democracy and those of the famous Liberal leaders of the past. I am sure that the great men I knew so well in my youth would have regarded the establishment of a Socialist State and the enforcement of the collectivist theory as one of the worst evils that could befall Britain.' At Streatham Mr Duncan Sandys wrote a letter to all the known Liberals in the constituency. There was, he maintained, virtually complete agreement on foreign policy among Liberals, Conservatives and the official section of the Labour Party. But this policy was repudiated by Mr Aneurin Bevan, who had the support of nearly half the Labour M.P.s.[7]

Though there is no evidence to show that appeals of this kind were successful, the controversy over which way Liberals should vote did have an important result: it split the Liberals. Leading members of the party, instead of pronouncing suitably lofty and vague sentiments about conscience—which would have done no harm—treated the question in a tactless precise way. The result was confusion.

[7] *The Times*, 23 May 1955.

First, there were those who advised Liberals to support the Conservatives. 'I believe', declared Lord Moynihan, 'that Liberals should not be afraid to come down openly on one side or the other when they have no candidate of their own, and since the wrong side definitely seems to me to be the Socialists, it is best for Liberals without a candidate to vote Conservative next Thursday.'[8] The Dowager Countess, second wife of David Lloyd George, announced that she would vote Conservative. Lord Salter came down heavily in favour of Liberals voting Conservative where there was no Liberal candidate.[9] Lady Violet Bonham Carter did not go so far as to recommend voting Conservative: but she was passionately anti-Socialist. And Lord Samuel, in a speech at the National Liberal Club—the best-publicised Liberal speech of the election—was notably ill-disposed towards Labour. 'Remembering the past,' he said, 'and looking at the Labour manifesto now issued, I for one should feel the greatest anxiety for the economic stability of the country if this election were to give absolute control of the House of Commons to Labour . . . It is now plain that the Labour Party is morally and intellectually on the decline.'[10]

Then there were those who recommended voting Labour: Lady Megan Lloyd George, of course (who had joined the Labour Party three weeks previously) and Mr Dingle Foot.

Finally there were suggestions as to how the dictates of conscience could best be satisfied. A memorandum dispatched by Liberal headquarters to Liberal associations put forward the ideas that both Labour and Conservative candidates should be invited to attend a Liberal meeting, there to be asked 'leading Liberal questions'. The Liberal vote would depend on the answers received.[11] Very much the same approach was recommended by the *News Chronicle*, which 'urged its readers to hear and question their candidates, seeking those of informed and independent mind. These are the people, from whatever parties they may come, who will be most needed in the next Parliament. That, in our view, is the test: that is the way to decide how to vote.'[12] This agreed

[8] ibid. 24 May 1955.
[8a] *Daily Express*, 19 May 1955.
[9] Letter in the *Guardian*, 18 May 1955.
[10] Speech on 10 May.
[11] *The Times*, 11 May 1955.
[12] Leader, *News Chronicle*, 25 May 1955.

with Lord Rea's view[13]: but a pleasantly unorthodox note was struck by the Liberal Party handbook. Following the impeccable advice that one should have a strong reason for voting for either party, the handbook told of 'at least one Liberal' who was going to put in the ballot box, quite separately from his ballot paper, 'a slip something like this—my second preference is on the ballot paper; my first preference is proportional representation and fair opportunities for all opinions'.

The significance of this dispute is that it demonstrated three things, all interconnected, about the state of the Liberal Party at the time. First, the party lacked strong leadership at the top: for it is inconceivable that any self-respecting political organization, however dedicated it might be to the principles of freedom, would have allowed the expression of such varied views immediately before a general election. Second, many leading Liberals lacked any sense of political discretion. Third, and most important, the party had still not found its soul; it was still not clear about the direction in which it wanted to travel. And, when the votes were counted, it was apparent that the electors remained unimpressed. Liberal representation in the House stayed constant at six. There were sixty lost deposits, compared to sixty-six in 1951. The total number of votes polled by Liberals was 722,405 (in 1951 the figure was 736,556). The percentage share of the poll, however, went up from 2·5 to 2·7. There was, in short, no sign of the promised land. The small band were still in the desert, some of them plodding in one direction, some in another. But the green fields and cooling streams were as far away as ever.

What was to be done? The first organizational step which the party took was to set up a committee to lay plans for the next general election.[14] The Committee announced the beginning of a series of summer schools for candidates at the election. Whatever the value of this, the setting up of the committee so soon after the election did indicate a certain optimism in the party. And the Torquay by-election, which took place on 16 December 1955, was

[13] *The Times*, 24 May 1955.

[14] The Committee's members were: Sir Andrew McFadyean (chairman); Mr Jeremy Thorpe, prospective candidate for North Devon; Mr John Baker, Liberal Party Council; Mrs Whitamore, National Women's Liberal Foundation; Mr Edwin Malindine, Liberal Candidates' Association; Mr J. Walter, Liberals; and Mr R. Douglas, Chairman, National League of Young Liberals.

an encouraging enough result. There was life in the Liberal Party yet. The figures were[15]:

F. M. Bennett (Conservative)	20,964
W. Hamling (Labour)	10,383
P. J. Bessell (Liberal)	9,775
Conservative maj.	10,581

Two months later, in the Hereford by-election, Mr Frank Owen polled 9,979 votes, and pushed Labour into third place. And there were similarly encouraging results in the Taunton and Gainsborough by-elections. The average changes in percentages of the poll for these three by-elections were:

	1955	1956
Conservative	53·2	45·8
Labour	36·3	37·1
Liberal	10·5	17·2

Another encouraging sign for the party was the return to the fold of the Radical Reform Group, those Liberals who believed in the 'leavening of purely economic aims by some social priorities'. Private enterprise, the Group maintained, should to a certain extent work within a framework of State supervision. After the 1954 Assembly the Group had dissociated itself from the party, though individual members remained active, some as Liberal candidates. By 1956 it was felt that developments in party policy made reunion possible. Accordingly Mr Owen, the hero of Hereford, was adopted as Group vice-president.[16] Mr Desmond Banks, the Group's chairman, followed this up with some friendly remarks—and a clear indication of the way in which party policy ought to develop. If there were no Liberal Party, said Mr Banks, 'we might well be witnessing today the growth of some dangerous movement akin to that of M. Poujade in France. The existence of the vigorous Liberal Party ensures that present dissatisfaction with Tory ineptitude and Labour squabbling can find the positive outlook through a political movement which exists to reconcile individual

[15] The figures at the General Election were: Con. 29,777; Lab. 12,547; Lib. 7,012.

[16] *News Chronicle*, 23 February 1956.

freedom with that measure of wise planning which maintenance of our welfare society demands'.[17]

But this was the brighter side of things. On the other side, Lady Megan was followed into the Labour Party by Mr Dingle Foot, who took with him Mr Wilfred Roberts and Mr Philip Hopkins. Mr Foot tried to take with him also Mr Geoffrey Acland: but Mr Acland would have none of it; more, Mr Acland told all. It was imperative in the interests of the party, he said, to make it known that he had been approached by Mr Foot to join the Labour Party. To expect him to adopt such a course, said Mr Acland, was nothing more than an indication of the extent to which some people had lost contact with what the Liberal Party was doing and saying. There would always be 'those who will seek excuses to align themselves with one or other of the second-best alternatives, in order more speedily to fulfil their political ambitions'.[18]

Nor was it only the Left which won converts from the Liberal Party in this period. There was also a trickle in the direction of the extreme *laissez-faire* Right, as represented by Mr Edward Martell's union-busting People's League for the Defence of Freedom. Though, judging by Mr Martell's subscription lists, the League drew most of its strength from the fixed-income Colonels and their ladies in the Southern coastal resorts, there was nevertheless a number of prominent ex-Liberals in the upper echelons of his organization. In the *Liberal News* of 21 September 1956 there appeared a full-page advertisement for the League. It proudly proclaimed that Mr Martell, the chairman, held a number of offices in the Liberal Party from 1945 to 1951; that Lord Moynihan, the treasurer, was chairman of the party in 1949-50; that Major H. E. Crawford had been Liberal M.P. for West Walthamstow; and that Mr Brian Goddard was national organizer of the Liberal Party from 1945 to 1948. The Liberal Party felt it necessary to counter this advertisment in the same issue of the *News*. The true League for the defence of freedom, went an announcement, was the Liberal Party itself. Any diversion of money and effort to any other organization was a weakening of the campaign for true Liberal purposes.

What was happening, in reality, was that the Liberal Party was

[17] Speech at Ruan Minor, Cornwall. ibid. 5 March 1956.
[18] ibid. 30 June 1956.

slowly and painfully finding a new purpose. It was shedding its extreme Left and its extreme Right. It was ceasing to be a doctrinaire party of free-trade, or proportional representation, or anything else. As the peace made by the Radical Reform Group showed, the party had come round to accepting some degree of State intervention in the economy. The mood for change was there all right. But where was the man? Clement Davies stayed on as leader, ailing and ineffective. Mr Attlee resigned from the leadership of the Labour Party, to be succeeded by Hugh Gaitskell. Churchill gave up the Conservative leadership, and Sir Anthony Eden took over. But Davies showed no sign of being prepared to go; and criticism of him grew both inside and outside the party.

However, there was nothing that could be done about Davies: as party officials pointed out, the Leader of the Liberal Party was elected by the Liberal M.P.s; and, if the M.P.s did not choose to do anything, no one could force their hand. Davies, it was devoutly hoped, would soon take one of the many hints that were in circulation, and do the decent thing. In fact he delayed until the Folkestone Assembly in September. And, until the end of the Assembly, there was no certainty in the minds of the delegates that Davies would indeed be departing. But there was little doubt about whom they wanted to succeed him. On 28 September 1956, when Mr Grimond rose to address the Assembly, delegates stood and applauded loudly for a full minute. Amid the loud cheering one fervent delegate was heard to cry: 'The hope of the Liberal Party.'[19] On the next day Davies finally took his leave, employing nautical terms for the purpose. 'It is time,' he said, 'that the tiller was placed in the hands of a younger man, and that a new voice should be calling on the ship's company, rallying them to the great cause which we all have so much at heart. Fortunately, I can step down knowing that there is a worthy successor waiting—one who has fully earned his master's certificate.'[20] Davies was warmly and lengthily cheered: one suspects that gratitude for his past services and relief at his decision to step down were mixed in about equal proportions. In the Press there was a sad paucity of tributes to Davies's leadership, though this may well have been because he was retiring not from political life—he remained M.P. for Mont-

[19] *Star*, 28 September 1956.
[20] *Guardian*, 1 October 1956.

gomery until 1962—but simply from the party leadership. At any rate, most of the attention was given to Mr Grimond. The unanimous verdict was that, if anyone could save the Liberal Party, here was the man to do it.

Mr Grimond's first test was the Suez crisis. The Liberals, like the other two parties, were divided in their attitude towards the Government's action. The difference was, however, that the major parties succeeded in concealing their splits considerably better. On 30 October 1956 Davies, Mr Wade and Mr Holt entered the Division Lobby on the Government side and in support of the ultimatum to Egypt. Two days later, on a Labour motion deploring the action taken in Egypt, the Liberals present voted for the motion and against the Government. According to Lord Rea, the party's leader in the Lords, the reason for the first vote was that the Liberals believed the Commonwealth and the Western allies had been consulted about the Government's action.[21] Though this may well have been the explanation for the votes of Mr Davies and Mr Wade, it can hardly have applied to Mr Holt. For, after it was made clear that the Commonwealth and the Western Allies had not in fact been consulted, Mr Holt's 'own personal view is that in an extremely awkward and grave situation, the action of the Government is justified . . .'[22] And there were plenty of other Liberals who shared Mr Holt's sentiments. There were Sir Oscar Hobson, Mr Howard Fry, Mr John MacCallum Scott and Mr Peter Cadbury. Even Lord Samuel seemed to give aid and comfort to the Government: 'Britain and France,' he said on 30 October 1956, 'had adopted the usual course on the part of bystanders of trying to keep the combatants apart, which, as an immediate measure, was the most sensible thing to do.'[23]

One should not be too hard on the Liberals for their varying attitudes over Suez. It was a confused and emotional period. Those who opposed the Government's action did so for differing and often contradictory reasons. In the Labour Party there was a clear conflict of approach between Gaitskell and Bevan, between the high-minded and the hard-minded, between the heirs of Gladstone and the heirs of Bright.[24] Mr Richard Crossman went so far as to

[21] Letter in *The Times*, 25 September 1959.
[22] *Bolton Evening News*, 3 November 1956, quoted D. Llewellyn, M.P., letter in *Daily Telegraph*, 17 September 1959.
[23] See D. Llewellyn, M.P., loc. cit.
[24] cf. A. J. P. Taylor, *The Trouble Makers* (1957), p. 189.

suggest that the Government should have let the Israeli armies go ahead and inflict a crushing defeat on Egypt.[25] Thus the Liberals were not alone in their confusion. And they soon remedied it. On 2 November 1956 the Liberal Party organization issued a statement which unequivocally condemned the Government's action.[26] Four days later the parliamentary party fell into line: the Liberal Party Committee (which is appointed by the Leader, and responsible for co-ordinating policy decisions between the parliamentary party and the Liberal Party Organization) endorsed the organization's statement.[27]

From then on, though there was the odd dissentient voice, the Liberal Party fought the Conservatives with a vigour which had not been seen since the war. Mr Grimond was clearly taking a risk. With the exception of himself, all the Liberal M.P.s had been allowed a clear run in their constituencies against the Labour candidate. Suppose the Conservative Party withdrew its concession? What would happen then? The question was soon put to the test. Sir Rhys Hopkin Morris, the widely-respected Liberal Member for Carmarthen, died. Sir Rhys had held the seat in straight fights against Labour. Now the Conservatives threatened to cancel the agreement in the forthcoming by-election, and contest the seat themselves. What ought Mr Grimond to do?

In the event he compromised. Though Liberal attacks on the Government did not abate, a candidate was chosen for Carmarthen who was in favour of the Suez operation; and the Conservatives did not put up a rival. The Labour candidate was appropriately enough Lady Megan Lloyd George. Mr J. Morgan Davies, the Liberal choice, made his views clear. 'Britain and France', he said, 'halted the spread of hostilities in the Middle East. The real enemy of mankind is the Soviet Union, which is being led by evil men.'[28] Mr Grimond's views on Suez, at least as vouchsafed to the voters of Carmarthen, were considerably less clear: when he spoke on Mr Davies's behalf he did not once mention the subject. All this was too much for Miss Honor Balfour, a founder of the old Radical Action movement and a member of the Liberal Executive. She resigned from the party, accusing it, in a letter to Mr Grimond,

[25] 560 H. C. Deb. 5s., 860 (13 November 1956).
[26] *News Chronicle*, 3 November 1956.
[27] *The Times*, 7 November 1956.
[28] Speech at Carmarthen, 12 December 1956, quoted D. Llewellyn, M.P., loc. cit.

of compromising over Suez to win Conservative votes.[29] Miss Balfour was out of the party and Lady Megan was in the Commons. Liberal representations in the House was at five, the lowest since the war.

And yet there was not as much despondency as there might have been. The truth was that many members of the party, those who were not prepared to go to the lengths of Miss Balfour, were slightly ashamed of the Carmarthen episode. Was not the defeat of Mr Davies by Lady Megan a blessing in disguise? Would he not have been an embarrassing reminder, sitting there in the third bench back below the gangway, of what was, after all, an incident in the history of the party that was best forgotten? For, the Carmarthen by-election apart, Suez had given the Liberals the opportunity to show themselves as a vigorous fighting party. Moreover, Suez had done something else. It had, in a curious way, activated British politics. It had exorcised the ghost of Butskellism. It had convinced people hitherto uninterested in, or downright hostile to, politics, that public opinion could still affect the actions of Governments. In Gladstone's phrase, 'the general sentiment of the civilized world' had prevailed. Or, at least, this is what many people in Britain thought had happened. Whether the retreat from Suez really owed more to Mr Khrushchev's rocket-rattling, or to Dulles's hostility towards Sir Anthony Eden, is for this purpose immaterial. Suez convinced the Liberals that British Governments could be wicked, or foolish, or both; and it convinced the Liberals that something could be done to remedy this. One beneficiary of this new mood was the Labour Party, which, though it lost a number of sixpence-a-week working-class members, gained middle-class activists. And another beneficiary was Mr Grimond.

Mr Grimond perceived, in the year which followed Suez, that an interest in political issues could go together with a distaste for activities of the major parties. The people of Britain, he told the Southport Assembly in September, were reacting against the two-party, two-class struggle. A new, uncommitted generation was growing up. The rising scientists and technicians, the new artisans, were 'neither Tory nor trade union fodder'. The Tories, said Mr Grimond, had no vision of the sort of society these people wanted. But Liberals could not accept Socialist solutions. It was partner-

[29] *News Chronicle*, 25 February 1957.

ship, not nationalization, that the workers required in industry.[30] Certainly 1957 saw a marked Liberal resurgence. The year that began with the defeat of the Liberal candidate at Carmarthen ended with the 1922 Committee of the Conservative Party clamouring for stronger measures to be taken against the Liberal peril. For the by-election results were surprisingly encouraging. In May Mr William Douglas-Home polled 7,438 votes in the South Edinburgh by-election. 'The most encouraging advance for the party since Mr Jo Grimond became leader', commented the *Guardian*.[31] 'If Liberals in other parts of Britain follow this lead,' said the *Evening Standard* of 30 May 1957, 'then Mr Douglas-Home may one day find himself in his brother's place as Secretary of State for Commonwealth Relations. And the change might not be a bad one. Certainly Mr William Douglas-Home could not commit more indiscretions than his brother, the 14th Earl of Home.' South Edinburgh was followed by the Gloucester by-election, where Lieutenant-Colonel Patrick Lort-Phillips won 7,393 votes. Mr Grimond said on television that the country might have a Liberal Government in ten years.[32] And then came the Ipswich by-election, which Mr Dingle Foot won for Labour, but in which the unorthodox and newsworthy Miss Manuela Sykes came a creditable third, with 12,587 votes. At the Southport Assembly an appeal for funds brought in £11,889 in an hour.[33] It was announced that party membership had increased by 30,000 in the previous twelve months—about 5,000 more than the gain in the year before that.[34] And Mr Grimond said that 'the old life-buoys which have kept this party afloat so long are dropping astern and in the next ten years it is a question of get on or get out, and let us make it get on'.[35] Mr Grimond had decided to aim as high as he could. Though there were suggestions, in the press and in the party, that the Liberals should confine themselves to the role of a pressure-group, Mr Grimond was determined to seek political power. And, whatever right-wing Liberals such as Mr. John MacCallum Scott might say, Mr Grimond was determined to do this as a Radical.

One indication of the way things were going was the party's nuclear policy. While the Labour and Conservative parties sup-

[30] *Observer*, 22 September 1957.
[31] *Guardian*, 31 May 1957.
[32] ibid. 18 September 1957.
[33] *The Times*, 23 September 1957.
[34] ibid. 3 September 1957.
[35] *Daily Telegraph*, 23 September 1957.

ported the retention of the independent deterrent, the parliamentary Liberal party, in March 1957, stated that Britain should give up the separate manufacture of nuclear weapons and concentrate on nuclear research. The general pattern of defence should be a contribution of conventional arms to NATO and a mobile reserve. What was needed was a highly-trained regular army of 100,000-175,000.[36]

The statement was perhaps as significant a clue as any kind of leadership which Mr Grimond was beginning to offer the party. For the nuclear policy was not only ahead of its time: it was also symbolic of the growing separation of Liberal policy from Conservative. In April 1958 it was made clear that the Liberals would play no part in 'keeping the Socialists out'. The party Executive issued a statement to this effect. The Liberal Party, went the statement, was so busy in its essential work of promoting Liberalism that it had no time for keeping others out of Parliament: neither the Liberal Party nor any other party had the right to deprive the electors of the free choice to vote as they thought fit: Conservative Central Office and Transport House had far more in common with each other than with the Liberals: it was precisely Conservative-held marginal seats which furnished the best opportunity for Liberal gains: if the Macmillan Government was genuine in its fear of Socialism it could prove its sincerity by introducing electoral reform: an anti-Socialist front would consolidate Socialism for half-a-century: the true issue politics was Liberals v. anti-Liberals.[37]

All hope of alliances was gone: the Liberal Party was determined to go its own way. And indeed this fact had already been perceived by the Conservatives. With Central Office approval, the habit grew of referring to the 'independent Liberals'. Lord Hailsham, the Conservative Party Chairman, was loud in his condemnations. The Liberal Party, he said, had 'no aim for the country except to be governed by itself, no philosophy, no outlook, and no ideas which have not been at least as effectively voiced by ourselves'.[38] The day following this outburst the Liberal Party Council passed a resolution calling for the largest possible number of candidates at the general election. The Council considered that the

[36] Statement of 28 March 1957.
[37] Liberal Party Executive Statement, 12 April 1958.
[38] Speech at Glasgow, reported *Daily Express*, 15 February 1958.

election would provide the party with 'its finest opportunity for 30 years'. Therefore the Council urged all Divisional Liberal Associations to make immediate efforts to fight the election.[39] Lord Hailsham, for his part, continued to bubble with indignation at the Liberals. 'In actual practice,' he said, 'a vote for the Liberal candidate is only another way of voting for the Socialists. It is not my idea of democracy that the smallest party should be allowed to determine the fate of the other two. Sooner or later the Liberals will have to come down to realities. I hope they will do so before they have done any more mischief.'[40]

What had alarmed Lord Hailsham, and the rest of the Conservative leaders, was the success of Liberal candidates in the by-elections. At Rochdale in February Mr Ludovic Kennedy came within 4,530 votes of winning the seat; and the Conservative finished up at the bottom of the poll. Mr Kennedy exceeded in glamour possibly even Mr Robin Day (who became the general election candidate for Hereford): for Mr Kennedy was tall, dark, Etonian and married to the ballet-dancer Miss Moira Shearer. Though there was some doubt as to the length of time for which he had been a member of the party—'I find,' he said, 'that since I have been a subscriber to the *Liberal News* for eighteen months I have been automatically a member of the party for eighteen months.'[41]—there could be no questioning his attractiveness as a candidate. The result at Rochdale was:

J. McCann (Labour)	22,133
L. H. C. Kennedy (Liberal)	17,603
J. E. Parkinson (Conservative)	9,827
Labour Majority	4,530

Inside the Conservative Party there were mutterings to the effect that every Liberal should be opposed by a Conservative at the general election. Rochdale, however, was only a beginning. The Conservative and National Liberal Member for Torrington, Mr George Lambert, was elected to the peerage following the death of his father, the aged Lord Lambert. At that time a Bideford

[39] *Observer*, 16 February 1958.
[40] Speech at Weston-super-Mare, reported *The Times*, 10 June 1958.
[41] *Daily Express*, 8 January 1958.

farmer, Mr Ambrose Fulford, was Liberal candidate for the seat. But the seat could be won—it had returned a Liberal Member before 1931, when Lord Lambert became a National Liberal—and there were Liberals who doubted whether Mr Fulford was quite the man to win it. Accordingly Mr Fulford was constrained to withdraw as candidate. 'The most generous and magnanimous action I have ever known in politics', declared Mr Herbert Harris, the general director of the party.[42] And at a selection conference Mr Mark Bonham Carter defeated Mr John Foot for the Liberal nomination.

Mr Bonham Carter, the son of Lady Violet, was a London publisher. Before Suez there had been rumours that he might join the Conservatives, when he would have been a welcome convert: for, with Mr Byers and Mr Grimond, he was one of the few politicians in the Liberal Party who were in the very highest class. Indeed there were many who thought that, though he lacked Mr Grimond's charm—Mr Bonham Carter was ascetic in appearance and slightly didactic in manner—he had an altogether keener political brain than his leader. By 1958 all prospects of his joining the Conservative Party had gone; and Mr Bonham Carter fought a hard campaign on bread-and-butter issues. The result was:

M. R. Bonham Carter (Liberal)	13,408
A. H. F. Royle (Conservative)	13,189
L. Lamb (Labour)	8,697
Liberal Majority	219

There was a torchlight procession through Bideford and a luncheon at the National Liberal Club. Lady Violet Bonham Carter was quite overcome by it all. 'I had the strange sense', she confessed, of being a member of an army of liberation entering occupied country which for years had been ruled by Quislings and collaborators and that their day was over once and for all. There are in England thousands of Liberals living in occupied territory whom we have got to liberate.'

The Liberal victory at Torrington was no doubt glorious: but it was hardly as glorious as all that. At least one of the public opinion polls had forecast a win for Mr Bonham Carter; and

[42] ibid. 23 February 1958.

locally Liberals were confident of a majority of more than 219. Yet it would be difficult to exaggerate the effect of the Torrington result on Liberal morale. Suddenly, it seemed, the long years of waiting had become worthwhile. For the first time since 1929 the Liberal Party had actually won a seat. The revival was no longer on its way: it was here. Mr Grimond looked forward to forty Liberal Members holding the balance in the new House of Commons;[43] and Mr Bonham Carter laid down a target of not fewer than eight seats in the West Country.[44]

Nor, at this time, was their confidence entirely without foundation. Nineteen fifty eight was, as 1962 was later to be, a great Liberal year. March 1958 was the month not only of Torrington but also of the Gallup Poll in which 33 per cent answered Yes to the question: 'If you thought that the Liberals would get a majority, would you be likely to vote for them?' This figure of 33 per cent was soon to assume, in Liberal eyes, an almost mystical significance: certainly it was more quoted by Liberals than any other statistics of the post-war period.[45] Two months later there was perhaps more solid reason for hope in the local elections in which the Liberals made a net gain of 79 seats.

What was the explanation of the Liberal resurgence? Spokesmen for the major parties were in little doubt. The Liberals were Poujadist, irresponsible, neo-Fascist; they had no policy and no leaders. Lord Hailsham was in familiar voice; and Morgan Phillips, Secretary of the Labour Party, diagnosed 'an unhealthy tinge in this new "Liberalism" with its victory torch parades and irresponsible appeal to the self-interest of the lower middle classes. I have not the slightest doubt that the so-called Liberal revival has so far been carried through entirely because of its escapist appeal.'[46]

And in a sense Phillips and Lord Hailsham were quite right. The leading Liberal activists and the Liberal voters were marching in different directions. Mr Grimond, Mr Byers and Mr Bonham Carter saw Liberalism in terms of economic growth and international co-operation, of wider property ownership and greater diffusion of power within the State. An ambundance of speeches and policy documents testified to the steadfastness, if not always to the clarity,

[43] J. Grimond, *The New Liberal Democracy* (1958).
[44] Speech at Barnstaple, reported *The Times*, 5 May 1958
[45] See *News Chronicle*, 17 March 1958.
[46] Labour Press Service, quoted *Daily Telegraph*, 31 May 1958.

of their purpose. This purpose was entirely different from anything in the minds of the majority of Liberal supporters. To them, Liberalism was essentially against something: against bureaucracy, or against Suez, or against party discipline, or even against the Bomb (though Liberal nuclear policy was not generally appreciated). A convert to the Liberal Party wrote that 'I am neither a Poujadist, neo-Fascist nor a sulky reactionary. I have been a life-long Tory but have joined the Liberal Party as a protest to (sic.) the pink Socialism of the present Conservative Government. I believe that the new Liberal Party is the spearhead of a liberating army. This nation cannot hope to recover its past greatness until it can throw off the dead hand of bureaucracy and rid itself of its parasitic professional politicians.'[47]

At this time, in the days after Torrington, there was a disposition on the part of both Liberals and non-Liberals to believe that sentiments such as those just quoted were confined to rank-and-file Liberal supporters; or, at most, to the lower echelons of the party. Mr Grimond had succeeded, to a considerable extent, in giving the impression that at the top the Liberals were progressive and youthful and up-to-date. But the Torquay Assembly showed that this impression was a misleading one: the Liberal old guard, it appeared, were full of fight. Or, if indeed they were dead, they were resolutely refusing to lie down. The Assembly's chairman was the aged Sir Arthur Comyns Carr, whose belief—understandable in one whose politics had been learnt in pre-electrical times—was that his voice could carry without the aid of a microphone. This belief was not well-founded. The chairman's requests and commands were for the first few days of the Assembly largely inaudible. The result was even more confusion than there would otherwise have been.

But the real fault did not lie in Sir Arthur Comyns Carr. It lay, first, in procedural errors, such as debating minor amendments at length while the substantive resolution went by default.[48] Second, and more important, the party was still not united in support of Mr Grimond's brand of Liberalism.

On free trade, for example, Mr Oliver Smedley moved a resolution on 'peace through trade'. He told delegates of the 'dynamic power of the Liberal Party's policy of unilateral free trade as a

[47] Sir Walter Fergusson Hannay, letter in *Daily Telegraph*, 26 April 1958.
[48] cf. *The Times*, 22 September 1958.

means to abolishing international tensions and promoting world peace'. An amendment sought to delete the words 'the Liberal Party's policy of unilateral. . . .' However, Mr Deryck Abel, the chairman of the executive, said that four or five post-war assemblies had committed the party to the idea of international free trade action. Whereupon Miss Claire Graham, the young prospective candidate for Skipton, declared that she had been brought up a Liberal free trader, and a free trader she remained. Free trade, in her view, was the most important principle of Liberalism. Miss Graham then turned her attention to the National League of Young Liberals and the League of University Liberals, both of which she accused of harbouring deviationists. 'I do not,' she said, 'want to wake up one morning to find I am a member of a party of disgruntled, conscience-stricken Tories and half-baked Socialists.' The Assembly dissolved in uproar.[49]

Again, on a resolution calling for an end to Britain's independent manufacture of the H-bomb, Sir Andrew McFadyean, a vice-president of the party and the chairman of its foreign affairs committee, said that 'there is something like hysteria about all this . . . If you want to end this country, make it quite clear that you are not going to make or use H-bombs'. About twenty voted with Sir Andrew, including Lord Grantchester (a party treasurer) and Mr Harold Glanville (the president-elect).[50] What was significant, however, was not the opposition to official policy by a number of leading party members. It was the fact that many of those who took part in the debate seemed completely unaware of what the party's nuclear policy was, even though it had been promulgated many times during the previous year.

And so it went on. On education, on agriculture, on party organization, there was not only dissent but—what was much worse—muddle and confusion. The 1958 Liberal Assembly was not a success.

It was left to Mr Grimond to retrieve something from the wreckage. In his address to the Assembly he was concerned to correct the impression that the party was, despite all the talk about youth, still being run by old men. Mr Grimond chose to deliver a vigorously-phrased attack on the honours system. 'The machines which dominate our policies,' he said, 'wield a great deal of their

[49] ibid. 20 September 1958.
[50] *News Chronicle*, 19 September 1958.

power through the amount of patronage which they can dispense. Peerages, life peerages, knighthoods, directorships, perquisites of every sort are showered on those whom the Prime Minister chooses to honour. The first thing that wants doing is to burst open patronage and privilege by which the Socialists and Tories manipulate our politics and maintain their rigid, out-of-date party structure. If we are going to preach democracy, let us practise it. Far too many prizes in the law, the Church, commerce and social life go to those whom the ruling clique find agreeable. Why, to enable us to have a second chamber, do we have to perpetuate the elaborate titles and absurd trappings of medieval barbarism? Time was when we laughed at Balkan princelings and South American generals with their strings of titles and their breasts full of medals, but today we are worse ourselves.'[51]

There ensued a brisk public correspondence between Mr Grimond and Lord Attlee over the award of honours. 'The issue,' wrote Mr Grimond, 'is not whether particular appointments or honours are well deserved; it is whether the system of which you approve should be continued.' Putting the Torquay Assembly behind him, Mr Grimond continued in the same Radical vein. A Liberal rally was organized at The Albert Hall by Mr Dominic le Foe, a bearded ex-professional magician who might well be described as one of the new men of Victoria Street. Mr le Foe laid on a searchlight, in whose beam leading Liberals were picked out on the platform (not always accurately). He also laid on the singing of 'Land of Hope and Glory'. 'Liberals,' said Mr Grimond, 'must give up being so excessively respectable. We have got to have some bloody noses in the party . . . The long-term objective is clear: to replace the Labour Party as the progressive wing of politics in this country, to sweep in not only Liberals but Liberal-Socialists and Liberal-Tories. It is certain that in the sixties a fresh tide will flow with new ideas and new leaders. I say to you that has got to be a Liberal tide.'[52]

The ultimate aim of replacing the Labour Party was to be repeated several times in the months that led to the 1959 election: thus Mr Grimond's strategy was fixed well before the quarrels which convulsed the Socialists in 1959-61.[53] The last thing that Mr

[51] Speech of 20 September 1958.
[52] Speech of 10 November 1958.
[53] See below, pp. 99f.

Grimond can be accused of is opportunism. Indeed the main charge which can be laid against him as a party leader is that he neither took nor made political opportunities. In the months that followed the Torquay Assembly there was no incident, no issue which sharply differentiated, in the public mind, the Liberals from the other two parties. Though the Liberals were five years ahead of Labour and Conservatives on such questions as the reform of Parliament and the modernization of industry, the bulk of the voters remained unimpressed. In politics it is almost as unprofitable to be early as it is to be late. And, above all, there was no second by-election comparable to Torrington. Though Liberal candidates put up creditable performances in the elections at Southend and Galloway, there was nothing to capture anyone's imagination.

Of course, Mr Grimond tried hard. His speeches were as aggressive as they had ever been. 'Britain today,' he said, 'is living in a stuffy, egotistical world of her own creation, worshipping the maces, wigs and paraphernalia of a political system to which neither Conservative nor Labour Party has given any thought whatever.'[54] But, somehow, all this seemed to be shadow boxing. The real enemy was not 'a political system' but Hugh Gaistkell, Mr Macmillan, the Labour Party, the Conservative Party; and the real enemy emerged unmarked from the attacks of the Liberals. In retrospect it is doubtful whether it could have been otherwise. As the election approached, so the process of polarization between Labour and Conservative continued. When the general election took place, Torrington had been extinguished as a beacon; instead it had passed into Liberal folk-lore.

[54] Speech at Liberal summer school, reported *News Chronicle*, 3 August 1959.

CHAPTER VI

THE ROAD TO ORPINGTON

I

THE general election of 1959 found the country in a curiously anti-political mood. Suez was only dimly remembered, even by those who had felt strongly about it. The killings at Hola Camp, indeed the whole African situation, had made little impact on the voters. Britain's independent deterrent, the Blue Streak, was at least a blue print: it had not been cancelled. The Conservative hero of the hour was Mr Macmillan. Had he not raised the standard of life of ordinary people to an unprecedented level? Had he not donned a fur hat in Moscow and saved civilization? The electors did not dissent. They returned the Conservatives with an increased majority.

And yet there were undertones of dissatisfaction. Aneurin Bevan had described the Parliament which had just been dissolved as 'the squalid Parliament'; the Conservatives were accused of selling their leader 'like a detergent'; the favourite word of abuse for the Government was 'cynical'. The Campaign for Nuclear Disarmament was gaining in strength; and earlier in the year the municipal workers' union, by coming out in favour of unilateralism, had begun that process which was later almost to destroy the Labour Party. The *Spectator* advised its readers to register their disgust by ignoring politics altogether; while its political writer, Mr Bernard Levin, pronounced Mr Grimond more intelligent, more honest and more handsome than the leader of either of the main parties.

In effect, Mr Grimond was seen by many people as a non-political leader. Inevitably his party gained something from the anti-political feeling which was in existence. And, though Mr Grimond did not go out of his way to court the anti-party vote, he tried to create the impression that the Liberal Party was different in kind from Labour and Conservative. In previous general elections the Liberals had claimed that they were the party of the middle, the party of reasonable men, the party not connected with 'vested interests'. In 1959 the emphasis was altered: the Liberals were Radical. And they were not only a party of the Left but a morally better party of the Left. On 3 October, in an appearance on television, Mr Grimond talked about the need for 'building up a new progressive radical party and at the same time getting politics back from the party machines into the hands of the people themselves'. In the Liberal manifesto *People Count*, which was published on 21 September, the main emphasis was not on policy but on a message from Mr Grimond deploring machine politics. 'The vote,' concluded the manifesto, 'does not belong to the Conservative and Labour Parties. It belongs to you.'

Not that policy was entirely ignored. *People Count* proposed improvements in the welfare services. It said that Britain should stop manufacturing nuclear weapons. And it was alone among the manifestoes in mentioning the control of trade unions. Indeed the Liberals, as on previous occasions, had plenty of policy: what was lacking was the resources, and the will, to put that policy across.

The lack of resources was freely admitted both by Liberal candidates and by headquarters. In fact there was a tendency to equate poverty with virtue. 'When I tell you,' wrote one candidate, 'that we had only three or four committee rooms for a constituency with eighty-one polling stations and no canvassing to speak of, then you will realize the extent of our achievement [they came second] . . . The remarkable thing was the high Liberal vote in spite of bad organization. As an example, [my colleague] was his own agent, had no active central committee room, put up his own posters, did his own loud-speaker announcements and held his press conferences with local reporters in a coffee bar, using the excuse that the campaign headquarters were too noisy with busy workers (of which, in fact, there were none). Yet he got second in the poll.'[1] Liberal window bills were scarce, cars even scarcer: of the 11 per cent of Liberals who had gone to vote in party cars, three-quarters said that the car was not a Liberal one.[2]

The paucity of resources, then, was clear. But what of the

[1] D. E. Butler and R. Rose, *The British General Election of 1959* (1960), p. 135. Many of the facts concerning the 1959 election are taken from this work.

[2] ibid. pp. 139, 142.

paucity of will? Certainly that was not so obvious: but it was nevertheless true that in the Liberal campaign there was something missing. One thing at least that was missing was Mr Grimond himself. He began the campaign by addressing a somewhat sparsely attended London rally on 15 September. Subsequently he retired to his constituency of Orkney and Shetland, leaving Liberal headquarters in the charge of Mr Frank Byers (the chairman of the campaign committee) and Mr Herbert Harris (the party's general director). Having regard to later happenings at Victoria Street[3] this cannot have been the most idyllic of partnerships. At any rate, Mr Byers and Mr Harris, hard though they worked, produced nothing resembling a national campaign. The Liberals appeared as the largest, and the least cranky, of the minor parties. If Mr Grimond had stomped the countryside the picture might have been different. It might even have been different if he had stayed in London and directed operations. But Mr Grimond sojourned for two weeks in his constituency—which he was hardly likely to lose—before embarking upon a one-day helicopter tour. Mr Macmillan, in a sixteen-day tour, made seventy-four speeches; Gaitskell, in thirteen days, made fifty-three.[4] Compared to these, Mr Grimond's effort was insignificant indeed.

Yet the result of the election was not wholly discouraging for the Liberals. True, Mr Grimond's prediction of eighteen to twenty seats, made a few months previously, was unfulfilled: Liberal representation in the Commons remained constant at six. True, Torrington, the party's proudest possession, went to the Conservatives: an emotional loss which was not entirely compensated for by Mr Jeremy Thorpe's win in North Devon. Nevertheless the Liberals had made an impact. They were still a force. They could, and did, claim that they had polled 6 per cent of the votes, but had won only 1 per cent of the seats. Further, of all the parties they alone had increased their percentage strength—in 1955 the Liberal share of the poll had been 2·7 per cent. They lost fifty-five out of 217 deposits, compared to sixty out of 109 in 1955. They came second in twenty-seven seats. And in North Cornwall, Bodmin, Torrington, Merioneth and Rochdale they obtained more than a third of the votes cast. In the ninety-one constituencies which they contested both in 1955 and in 1959 their total vote rose from 659,057

[3] See below, pp. 105ff.
[4] R. L. Leonard, *Guide to the General Election* (1964), pp. 130-1.

to 807,849.[5] Of these constituencies, there was a rise in support in the West Country, and a falling-off in the Celtic fringe.[6]

Perhaps because the Conservatives had done so unexpectedly well in the election, less than usual was heard about the Liberals 'splitting the vote' and 'letting the Socialists in'. Indeed it would have been difficult to point unwaveringly to any constituency where this had in fact happened. Oddly enough, however, Mr Harold Wilson took the view that the increase in the Liberal vote was due to disgruntled Conservatives voting Liberal. He was sharply corrected by Mr James Johnson, the defeated Labour M.P. for Rugby. 'This is not so,' wrote Mr Johnson, 'in our West Midland "affluent society", and in particular my constituency of Rugby. I want to warn him [Mr Wilson] that in the younger age groups, let us say the under-forties, there are large numbers of young men whose natural home at the polling booth is on the Left, but who are not voting Labour when they are offered a third candidate.' The reasons, according to Mr Johnson, were, first, objections to particular items in Labour policy and, second, the greater respectability of the Liberals.[7]

II

The voters to whom Mr Johnson referred were, of course, those to whom the Liberals' appeal was specifically directed. In the months that followed Labour's 1959 defeat the appeal was to grow in strength. As soon as the election was over, Mr Grimond said that Radicals could and must combine. The two main parties, he claimed, had fought the election on issues like the cost of living, pensions and the social services which did not really divide the nation. The true issues lay elsewhere: Mr Grimond said he was sure that a large block of opinion had opposed Conservative policies on matters of major importance, such as Suez, Cyprus and Africa. Politically, however, this block had been divided. He would like to see the Radicals—the Liberals and most of the Labour

[5] *Daily Telegraph*, 13 October 1959.

[6] In Montgomery the Liberal share went down by 26·1 per cent; Carmarthen, 15·2 per cent; Anglesey, 19·1 per cent; Cardigan, 6·2 per cent; Inverness, 5·8 per cent: Butler and Rose, op. cit. p. 233.

[7] Letter in the *Guardian*, 17 November 1959.

Party—make a new appeal to people 'to take a more active part in all sorts of real political issues'.[8]

What is interesting in this declaration is not its appeal to Radicals. It is the ambiguity with which this appeal was surrounded. Was Mr Grimond merely exhorting all sound Radicals to vote Liberal? Or was he suggesting some form of merger between the Labour Party and the Liberals (Labour's left wing having, in the meantime, been hived off)? And, if Mr Grimond was indeed contemplating a merger, how soon was it to be arranged? From the timing of Mr Grimond's remarks—they were made on the Saturday immediately following the general election—it is apparent that he was not soliciting votes. It was rather late in the day to be doing this. Most probably Mr Grimond was expressing an aspiration for the future. Certainly, as far as is known he made no kind of approach, whether formal or informal, to the Labour leadership. He perhaps lost a great opportunity.

Here it may be as well to turn aside for a moment and recollect the state of the Labour Party at this time. It is difficult now to recapture that particular mood of bitter self-questioning which reached its apogee at the Scarborough Conference of 1960. On the eve of that conference, in the lobbies and lounges of the Royal Hotel, men and women who had grown grey in the service of 'the movement' were openly expressing their doubts as to whether it could endure, at least in its existing form. These pessimists may not have been in a majority: but they were vocal; and even those who disagreed, such as Mr Richard Crossman, could look forward with apparent equanimity to ten years of Conservative rule.

In form, what divided the Labour Party was the attitude it should take to unilateral nuclear disarmament and to measures of further nationalization. The nationalization question was raised in an acute form by Hugh Gaitskell. He insisted that Clause IV—the clause in the party's constitution which laid down the public ownership of the means of production, distribution and exchange as an ultimate objective—was no longer appropriate; and he appeared somewhat surprised when he was attacked both by the fundamentalists and by the lovers of concord. In the event Gaitskell lost this battle; though practical proposals on nationalization remained moderate, as indeed they had been before the Clause IV question was raised. The whole episode was reminiscent of the

[8] Interview with M. Arnold-Forster, *Observer*, 11 October 1959.

Grand Old Duke of York: but, as so often happens in politics, an aura of the ridiculous made controversy the more bitter. The nuclear question, however, was altogether more serious, though here again the fundamental division was not so clear-cut as it was made to appear at the time. Following the cancellation of Blue Streak the Labour Party decided that Britain should not aspire to be a nuclear power—a policy which the Liberals had adopted two years earlier. The controversy became one of whether Britain should remain a full member of a nuclear-equipped Western Alliance. And here the Labour leadership finally triumphed.

But in essence the disputes of 1959-61 concerned the role of the Labour Party in British politics. How high a priority was to be attached to regaining office? Was the party to reflect the views of its activists or of its ordinary supporters in the country. As the memory of the 1959 defeat receded, and the Conservative Government's fortunes declined, so the prospect of power became more real. By the summer of 1961 the crisis was over.

During its existence the Liberals sometimes looked on loftily, sometimes gleefully cheered on both sides from the touchline. There was no offer of aid and comfort to Gaitskell. The Labour Party's affairs, the Liberals seemed to say, were its own business. If, by mishandling those affairs, Labour relinquished its position as principal opposition party, then so much the better . . . Though Mr Grimond continued to make predictions of the eventual pattern of British politics, he insisted that the first move towards a merger would have to come from the other side. He was content to point to 'the vacuum left in politics by the disintegrated Labour Party'[9] A merger would be a possibility 'if the Labour Party come to their sense and face facts . . . But it is up to them. This question is one the Labour Party has never answered. They really think that private enterprise is a wicked thing—or at least they give that impression. But they have got to come clean sooner or later and admit that a mixed economy is the only answer to today's problems. It is something which they will have to decide and which they will eventually have to agree upon with us. When they do that there is a chance that we could do it together.'[10]

For the moment, the Liberal aim was to become the principal party of radical opposition. Mr Grimond had to convince the pub-

[9] Speech at Stockport, *News Chronicle*, 19 March 1960.
[10] ibid. 6 February 1960.

lic that the Liberals were the alternative to the Conservatives. Nor was it only the public that he had to convince. He clearly felt that sometimes his own party was less than properly enthusiastic. Addressing the executive of the Woman's Liberal Federation, he warned his followers that they must make up their minds during the next few months whether they wanted to become the party of the 'new Left'. He suggested that he was getting tired of leading a party whose members relied upon others to 'carry on the fight'. It had been his hope, said Mr Grimond, that the Liberal Party would be at the heart of a new Left, attractive to many people in other parties and in none. He had no doubt that such a Left would emerge. What the Liberal Party had yet to show, however, was that it appreciated the present opportunity and could muster the enthusiasm to seize it. 'We must not only believe that the reforms we propose are right and practicable. We must be seen by the general public to be mad keen on them and to be campaigning effectively for them.'[11]

III

The first step towards effective campaigning was to formulate some coherent policy on the fighting of by-elections. There were at least three choices open to the Liberals. First, they could try to contest every by-election that came along. Second, they could contest those seats in which there was a prospect of putting up a reasonable performance. Or, third, the decision could be left to the local constituency organization. The formula which was in fact arrived at was a somewhat unsatisfactory combination of all three approaches.

For several years prior to the 1959 election Liberal policy had been to urge local associations to fight by-elections where certain minimum requirements relating to organization, finance and candidates were met.[12] This approach had been formally endorsed by the Liberal Party Council on 8 November 1957. It was re-affirmed by Mr Grimond at a meeting of the Council two years later. The Liberals, he said, would fight by-elections 'where there is a real local determination backed by local work, money and organiza-

[11] *Daily Telegraph*, 8 July 1960.
[12] See A. Holt, M.P., letter in the *Guardian*, 29 March 1960.

tion'.[13] In other words, Liberal headquarters would not force a local association to fight a by-election against the association's will: but headquarters would try to prevent a contest where local Liberal resources were inadequate. It is difficult to escape the conclusion that this solution managed, in a most ingenious fashion, to combine the disadvantages both of centralized control and of regional anarchy. On the one hand, there could be no question of a centrally directed by-election plan: the initiative was left to the local associations. But, on the other hand, any local Liberal party which showed too much initiative was liable to be told sternly to stop playing at politics. Liberal headquarters abrogated authority except in a limited class of cases: but when that authority was exercised it was bound to appear oppressive.

This may not have been satisfactory, but the principle—of local option, subject to a central veto—was fairly clear. Mr Grimond, however, then went boldly forward and introduced a different by-election principle: that of blanket coverage. He said that he wanted every constituency association to meet and consider whether it could fight a by-election. If the association decided it could not, it should fix a date by which it would be able to do so.[14] This was not all. The Liberal leader had another idea in the hat. He suggested a band of peripatetic Liberal candidates, a mobile *corps d'élite* of potential by-election winners. 'The point is,' said Mr Grimond, 'that a by-election might come along at any time in a constituency which was perhaps without a prospective Liberal candidate for the time being, but where we had a really good chance. If all our most promising candidates were already adopted for constituencies which they felt they could not leave, we might miss that chance. In the normal course of events a candidate sticks to his constituency and works it up. But in a party which put up only just over 200 candidates at the last election and hopes to put up more next time the pattern of candidature may change. We don't want it to be absolutely flat and rigid.'[15]

It should be remembered that this suggestion—and 'suggestion' is perhaps too weak a word—was made by Mr Grimond in almost literally the same breath as he had supported the policy of local choice over by-elections. Evidently he did not see any contradic-

[13] *The Times*, 16 November 1959.
[14] ibid.
[15] *Daily Telegraph*, 16 November 1959.

tion. But the trouble was surely this: the Liberals had not made up their minds about the basic approach. They never really decided whether the impetus should come, as it were, from below or above. Not too much need be made of this failure. It does not necessarily follow that more impressive results would have been achieved if a more clear-cut policy had been adopted. No doubt there was something to be said for Mr Grimond's flexibility of attitude. And, in any case, active politicians of all parties constantly over-estimate the importance of organizational patterns. As it turned out, only two by-elections produced serious embarrassments for the Liberal Party.

First there was Brighouse and Spenborough. Labour had held this seat with a majority of forty-seven at the 1959 election; and when the vacancy arose at the end of that year (owing to the death of Mr John Edwards) it seemed a good opportunity for the Liberal Party to try its strength. The *Guardian* in particular urged action. However, Liberal headquarters advised against putting a candidate in the field, and the Brighouse executive accepted that advice. Whereupon five officials of the association—the chairman, the treasurer, the secretary and two members of the executive—promptly resigned. These dissentients wrote that they felt there was no other course to adopt in view of the lack of support from headquarters. 'It seems,' they said, 'that party headquarters are totally uninformed about affairs in this constituency, where there exists a so-called United Liberal and Conservative Association who have named a Conservative as candidate.'[16] Headquarters replied that the decision not to fight was taken at a full meeting of the association, when only one person voted against and five abstained. The advice not to fight had been proferred, claimed headquarters, because the Brighouse Liberals could not fulfil the by-election tests of a reasonable standard of organization and sufficient funds. Further, it was always open to a local association to ignore the advice of headquarters.[17] In the event Brighouse remained unfought by the Liberals, and the Conservatives gained the seat from Labour with a majority of 666.

The trouble at Ebbw Vale, the second case of by-election difficulty, was quite different. For at Brighouse no reasonable candidate was in sight. At Ebbw Vale, on the other hand, the candidate

[16] *The Times*, 11 January 1960.
[17] ibid. 12 January 1960

was all too visible; and Liberal headquarters were not over-pleased with the sight. Lieutenant-Colonel Patrick Lort-Phillips, the hero of the Gloucester by-election, had occupied a temporary place in the Liberal pantheon. But in 1960 he was regarded as something of a trouble-maker. He possessed, and showed no reluctance to propogate, views on the nuclear deterrent which went far to the Left of official policy. And he had resigned from the party treasurership on account of the over-brisk headquarters reorganization which had taken place.[18] Colonel Lort-Phillips announced that Ebbw Vale must be fought—he was prepared to fight it—if the Liberals were to be taken seriously as an alternative to Labour. Had the Monmouthshire Liberal Federation decreed that Ebbw Vale should not be contested? Colonel Lort-Phillips was not in the least put out. The Monmouthshire Federation, he retorted, had no right to exist at all. 'In the Party constitution,' he said, 'this Federation does not exist. They are a group of well-meaning people and that's all'—a view to which the Secretary of the Liberal Party of Wales was constrained somewhat lamely to agree.[19] But there was another difficulty: in Ebbw Vale there was no Liberal Association. Here again Colonel Lort-Phillips was not disconcerted. He would create a Liberal Association. Alas, however, on this occasion the Colonel's gallantry went unrecognized. He came third in the poll (sandwiched between the Conservative and the Welsh Nationalist); and his percentage vote of 11·6 was the lowest of any Liberal in the pre-Orpington period.

A much more important decision had to be taken by the Liberals in respect of the vacancy at East Bolton. For here, ever since the 1951 election, the local Liberals and Conservatives had, by a series of electoral agreements, kept Labour out of both the borough's seats. The Conservatives had held East Bolton with Liberal support. And, in return, Mr Arthur Holt had been maintained as Liberal M.P. for West Bolton. Clearly, if the Liberals contested East Bolton they would, in effect, be serving notice that as far as they were concerned the era of Conservative-Liberal pacts was finally at an end. Nor was this the only consideration. East Bolton was an industrial constituency; a constituency moreover in which, unlike Ebbw Vale, there was a reasonable chance of a good Liberal vote. If they did not fight Bolton, the Liberal

[18] See below, pp. 105ff.
[19] *Daily Mail*, 22 August 1960.

leaders asked themselves, could they, did they deserve to be, taken seriously as the independent radical alternative to Labour? The leadership hesitated for many weeks, and then decided. East Bolton should be fought, and fought with a nationally known candidate. Mr Frank Byers was dispatched North from London. Mr Byers did not, as it turned out, do sensationally well. He came third in the poll with 10,173 votes (24·8 per cent). His campaign was scarcely helped by the *Liberal News*'s reference to his Conservative opponent, Mr Edwin Taylor ('the dancing pieman') as 'non-U'. Still, the decision to fight East Bolton was crucial. From that moment, the Liberal Party was seriously in business.

IV

Change was also discernible at party headquarters. Two months after the election a reorganization committee was set up. Its terms of reference were 'to improve as rapidly as possible the national, regional and constituency organization of the party and to strengthen the impact of Liberalism on the electorate'. Its members were Mr Frank Byers (chairman), Mr Arthur Holt, M.P., Mr Richard Wainwright, Mr Mark Bonham Carter and Mr Jeremy Thorpe, M.P.[20] This investigation had been promised by Mr Grimond immediately after the election; and the reorganization committee was evolved out of the campaign committee which had supervised the general election under Mr Byers.

On January 1960 the committee's recommendations were put before the Liberal Executive. Two days afterwards the Executive's findings were confirmed by the Liberal Council. Mr Douglas Brown, who was later himself to become a Liberal Party employee, had already tried to soften the blow by giving warning of what was to come. 'The sort of shake-up which seems inevitable,' he wrote, 'must have some painful consequences. The discussion of them must involve some personal antipathies. Liberals are as human as the rest. So it is no secret that there are conflicts to be resolved. But this is a new start . . .[21] The 'new start' involved dispensing with the post of General Director of the Party and—what need not necessarily have followed from this—dispensing with the then incumbent, Mr Herbert Harris. A new 'organization committee'

[20] *Daily Telegraph*, 14 December 1959.
[21] *News Chronicle*, 8 January 1960.

was to be set up, and the post of 'co-ordinating secretary' (i.e. chief of the Liberal Party machine) created. Meanwhile Mr Harris was to be thrust out on to the wide pavement of Victoria Street.

Mr Harris was not disposed to take this treatment without some form of public protest. He summoned a press conference. Here he made clear that, before the reorganization committee had begun its deliberations, Mr Byers had told him that he was unpopular with everyone and would have to go. Mr Harris agreed to discuss terms, but later withdrew. Of his last three weeks—the final day was 29 January—Mr Harris said: 'They were quite fantastic, if not comical. On my last day only Lord Grantchester called in. Unpopular! Had I been a leper, had I been guilty of some great offence, I could not have been more ostracised. I received no message from Mr Grimond.'[22]

Mr Harris was not entirely friendless. Mr R. A. Smith, who had been managing editor of the *Liberal News* since January 1951, resigned in protest. Mr Smith explained that he had done so—against the advice of Mr Harris—because it was inconceivable to him that a political party should put out a manifesto entitled *People Count* yet 'not make the utmost endeavour to retain in an honourable position in its new plans a man who has given seven years of such service as the Liberal Party has received from Herbert Harris'.[23]

Nor was this all. Mr Smith's resignation was followed by one from a more exalted position in the party: Lieutenant-Colonel Patrick Lort-Phillips relinquished his post of joint Treasurer. In his letter of resignation, Colonel Lort-Phillips maintained that the new organizing committee had taken over all the powers and responsibilities formerly attached to the treasurer's office. He had no function left. And, even if he did have a function, he did not have the means, the staff or the sources of information to perform it. Moreover, the reorganization committee had been set up without Colonel Lort-Phillips being informed or consulted: 'an action which was clearly designed to make my position untenable.'[24] Colonel Lort-Phillips went further. He had, he said, been 'expressly excluded from the committee . . . Mark Bonham Carter virtually runs the show'. The committee, said Colonel Lort-Phillips,

[22] *The Times*, 1 March 1960.
[23] ibid. 15 January 1960.
[24] ibid. 11 April 1960.

had not only selected itself and drafted its own terms of reference. It had also communicated its composition and terms of reference to the press before even the officers of the party had been informed of its existence. 'No one knows what they do. They don't publish any minutes.'[25] Colonel Lort-Phillips's changes went substantially uncorrected—though Mr Bonham Carter denied that he was the only operating member of the reorganization committee.[26]

Clearly not many potential Liberal voters were going to be swayed one way or the other by the news of the Palace revolution which was being carried through at Victoria Street. It was no concern of theirs if Mr Herbert Harris was cast into outer darkness or if Colonel Lort-Phillips decided that his role was as an independent Liberal deterrent. Rows in the Liberal Party are rarely news in the journalistic sense. To this extent Mr Grimond, aided by Mr Byers and Mr Bonham Carter, had greater freedom of manœuvre than would have been the case if he had been leading another party. He could afford to behave with a modicum of ruthlessness. The risk was of alienating the older-established, pre-Grimond elements in the party. As it turned out, these Liberals kept their heads well beneath the parapet. Most active party members relished the feeling of brisk and purposeful leadership. That this feeling was largely illusory[27] is not in this context important. Liberals felt that they were part of a tough, disciplined, new model electoral army. As Mr Grimond himself put it in his opening address to the Liberal Assembly of 1960: 'The Liberal Party has always demanded leadership. Well, you have had it. It has always been demanding better organization at headquarters. You have had that too. It was always demanding opportunity and you have got that now the ball is at your feet.'[28] And Mr Grimond was loudly applauded.

V

Indeed the way in which Liberal Assemblies were conducted throws an interesting light on changes in the party during the pre-Orpington period. Before the 1959 election the Assemblies were regarded as slightly comic events. Certainly no one outside the

[25] *Reynolds News*, 10 April 1960.
[26] *Daily Express*, 11 April 1960.
[27] For criticisms of by-election policy see above pp. 101ff.
[28] *Guardian*, 30 September 1960.

Liberal Party took them very seriously. The political correspondents treated them as an appropriately light-hearted introduction to the season, as an opportunity for limbering up before the really serious business—the Conservative and Labour Conferences, and the opening of the new parliamentary session. This particular branch of the entertainment industry probably put on its finest display at the 1958 Torquay Assembly.[29] Now all this was changed. The conference was planned by an agenda committee which in 1960, under the chairmanship of Mr Edwin Malindine, produced a plan for clear-cut debates on a limited number of subjects. Mr Malindine explained that the new procedure, which had been approved by the Liberal Council, had been adopted after an inquest on the 1958 Assembly. He assured delegates that, though some of their amendments might not have been accepted, they would nevertheless have a chance to air their views.[30] Mr Arthur Holt, M.P., when questioned about whether Liberals would take to such ruthlessness, replied that in the new mood of the party the only wish of the delegates would be to 'get on with the job'.[31] The same point was put in a slightly different way, and in private, by Mr Bonham Carter at the Eastbourne Assembly. 'God, what a bunch of masochists,' he said. 'They love the whip.' Miss Manuela Sykes, one of the few Liberals to whom the new order was not altogether congenial, quoted Mr Bonham Carter's observation and declared: 'Stalin is the only person who would be pleased with our progress.'[32]

VI

The Liberal Party, then, was to be an independent radical party. By-elections were, where possible, to be fought. Headquarters was to be better organized. The annual assemblies were to be more professionally run. All this, however, lacked the element of day-to-day contact with ordinary voters. To supply this, the Liberals decided to build up their strength in local government. 'Every time a local Liberal councillor gets a bus stop moved to a better place,' said Mr Grimond, 'he strikes a blow for the Liberal Party.'[33] And Mr Bonham Carter saw local activity as a way of laying the

[29] See above, pp. 99f.
[30] *The Times*, 14 September 1960.
[31] *Guardian*, 14 September 1960.
[32] *Liberal News*, May 1961.
[33] *Guardian*, 3 October 1960.

basis for solid support at parliamentary elections: 'It is easier to change people's voting habits at local elections than at by-elections and at by-elections than at general elections.'[34]

Throughout the pre-Orpington period the Liberals made steady and sometimes spectacular gains in local government. The total number of Liberal councillors rose from 475 to around 1,000. Where did these gains occur? Certainly there was nothing very sensational to report from Scotland, Wales and the West Country. The advances were made in and around London: at Aldershot, Finchley, Kingston, Maidenhead, West Ham and, of course, Orpington. Both the issues and the techniques used for getting out the vote varied from locality to locality. One generalization, however, may safely be made: the Liberals were quicker to seize upon and exploit local dissatisfactions than were the other two parties. Local government, the Liberals said, was about local affairs. In Finchley, for example, the Liberals first gained attention through their championing of the right of Jews to be members of the local golf club (whose premises were leased from the Council at a nominal rent). Success over this issue was followed by vigorous complaints about the inadequacies of the bus services, and by the running of 'pirate' buses. And, on top of this, considerable attention was paid to getting the names of local Liberals well-known, and to canvassing the voters thoroughly.[35]

The comparative success of the whole local government operation was owed largely to the efforts of two men, Mr Richard Wainwright and, in particular, Mr Pratap Chitnis.[36] Until he became Mr Lubbock's agent at Orpington, Mr Chitnis was in charge of local government matters at Liberal headquarters. An Anglo-Indian, educated at Downside, he joined the party in 1958; became a full-time agent in 1959; and, following the election, went to Victoria Street. Despite, perhaps because of, his youth—he was born in 1936—Mr Chitnis was after Orpington to assume legendary proportions. He fulfilled a need which all particular parties in Britain seem to feel: the need for at least one politician whose views on trends and swings and majorities can be listened to with respect, and a measure of awe. This necessity should be distinguished from the purely practical business of actually having, at

[34] Quoted in R. West, 'Liberal HQ', *Time and Tide*, 22 March 1962.
[35] See A. Howard, 'Foothold in Finchley', *New Statesman*, 16 August 1963.
[36] cf. J. Grimond, 'Vindicated at the Polls', *Time and Tide*, 17 May 1962.

party headquarters, a number of political technocrats. Rather it is a matter of a party being able to call upon a highly-placed member who, himself remote from controversial politics, can judge which winds are blowing in which directions. In the Conservative Party this role has recently been filled by Lord Poole; in the Labour Party by Mr Herbert Bowden. For the Liberals Mr Chitnis, though far junior to these two, performed the same function.

VII

But what of Liberal policy during this period? What was the ultimate object of the reorganization of headquarters and the disciplining of the Assembly and the fighting of elections? Of course it was unfair and untrue to say, as so many Labour and Conservative speakers did say, that the Liberals had no policy. If anything the trouble was that they had too much of it. As Mr Angus Maude once unkindly observed, one had to buy up almost the entire stock of the Liberal Bookshop to discover what the policy was. Nevertheless, in this period certain outlines are more clearly drawn than others, certain cries are more insistent, certain themes detach themselves.

First there was the Common Market. Here the Liberal Party was categorical. *Britain Must Join* was the title of a party pamphlet published on the eve of the House of Commons debate on Europe in July 1960 (which was, of course, over a year before the Macmillan Government decided to apply for membership of the Market). 'No failure of British post-war policy,' said the pamphlet, 'has been so spectacular or so disastrous in its results as that of British policy in Western Europe.'

Closely allied to the Liberal belief in the Market was a preoccupation with the state of British industry. In July 1961 a party statement on partnership for industry urged—in addition to membership of the Common Market—production targets, stronger action against monopolies and restrictive practices, and improved research and advisory services. The statement recommended the encouragement of some kind of labour mobility. It argued that any worker, skilled or unskilled, should have the right to change his craft at any age. And it suggested an eventual ceiling on wages and profits. 'The State, in the last resort,' went the document, 'must be prepared to act alone in the matter of pay ceilings,' though it was preferable that agreement should be reached with the T.U.C. and the Employers Federation. Five months later the Liberal Council urged the Government to set up an independent agency to decide the average percentage increases in wages, salaries and dividends which the economy could meet, and to set a limit beyond which additional payments would be contrary to the public interest.[37]

But perhaps the clearest, and most authoritative, account of Liberal policy in this period is to be found in a speech by Mr Grimond to a London rally of Young Liberals. He proposed:

(i) A central economic planning unit with executive powers but separate from a tax-gathering Treasury. This unit would make a plan for expansion and relate pay and profit increases thereto.

(ii) An industrial charter establishing the status of industrial workers and setting up organizations throughout industry to provide information for the national plan.

(iii) A reform of the social services to ensure that pensioners shared in national expansion and were not penalized by inflation.

(iv) Steps to control monopolies and break up restrictive practices.

(v) A reform of the tax laws so as to simplify them and take some weight off earnings.

(vi) An expansion of technical and university education.

(vii) A small committee to co-ordinate the activities of all Ministries broadly concerned with town and country planning. Areas like the South East and the North East would be treated as units for development.

(viii) The abandonment of the British nuclear deterrent.

(ix) The abolition of the death penalty.

(x) The freeing of the Left from associations which did it damage.[38]

No one could reasonably say, then—though many did—that the Liberal Party had no policy. Whatever opinions might be held about the merits of particular proposals, there is no doubt that they added up to a relevant political programme. Proportional representation, free trade and the taxation of land values were forgotten. Instead the note was one of brisk economic innovation.

[37] See F. Boyd in the *Guardian*, 11 December 1961.
[38] *Observer*, 3 December 1961.

Economic growth; a wages policy; a national plan; regional development; an expansion of higher education: two years later these were to become the small change of Conservative week-end speeches.

VIII

But at this time the Liberal intention was to replace Labour as the radical opposition party. To what extent was this aim fulfilled? In the 1960 by-elections Liberal candidates pushed Labour into third place at West Harrow, Carshalton, Ludlow, Petersfield and Tiverton; in 1961, at Moss Side, Manchester and Oswestry. Judged in these terms—of placings in the poll—Mr Grimond could perhaps afford to feel reasonably satisfied, at least in 1960. But when percentage changes in the polls are examined it can now be seen that the picture for the Liberals was not nearly so encouraging. Nor was the Labour performance nearly as bad as it was thought to be at the time. For in only three by-elections in 1960—Carshalton, Ebbw Vale and Mid-Bedfordshire—did the Labour candidate lose proportionately more votes than the Conservative. Throughout this year, true, the Liberals polled well. But the point is that at this of all times, when the Labour Party appeared set on a suicidal course, nevertheless the Liberals showed no sign of being able to take more votes from Labour than from Conservatives.

In 1961 the pattern became more pronounced. The Conservatives lost an even greater share of their vote; Labour lost slightly less; and the Liberal Party did even better. Oddly enough, this was seen both by the Liberal leaders and by some Socialists as proof of the Liberal claim to be the radical alternative to Conservatism. 'Look,' said the Liberals, 'the Government is unpopular'—for these were the days of the pay pause. 'Its supporters are disappearing. But are they voting Labour? Not a bit of it. They are voting for us. For we are the radical alternative.' But on the contrary, the Liberal Party was the Conservative alternative. It was the resting place for the voters who had lost faith in Mr Macmillan and his Government. These voters could stay Liberal, or move back to their former allegiance, or switch from Liberal to Labour. They could be joined by other former Conservatives. No one, at the end of 1961, could be blamed for making any of these predictions. Mr Grimond could justifyably be optimistic about the future. But the only prediction which could not rationally be made was that the Liberal Party would replace Labour.

IX

Mr Woodrow Wyatt, the Labour M.P. for Bosworth, did not go so far as to predict this. He was, however, worried about the ability of the Labour Party to defeat the Conservatives unless some electoral agreement with the Liberals could be arrived at. And Mr Wyatt was not alone. Ever since Labour was beaten into third place by the Liberal at the Oswestry and Moss Side by-elections, the possibility had been discussed by some Socialists. But Mr Wyatt's voice was the most insistent. Though Gaitskell formally knocked down the proposal at the annual dinner of the Bosworth Constituency Labour Party, though there were insistant demands for Mr Wyatt's expulsion, he stuck to his ideas with typical tenacity.[39] In 1906, he pointed out, the Labour Representation Committee won twenty-nine seats. This was owing to arrangements made between Labour and the Liberals. 'Of course some lily-white-pure Socialists at the time complained of the deal with the Liberals, preferring to wait for the millennium; but the practical realism of Keir Hardie and his associates triumphed'.[40] Besides, he wrote, in 1931 a secret argreement was made between Arthur Henderson and Lloyd George. Under this agreement Lloyd George urged Liberals in constituencies where no Liberal candidate was standing to vote for Labour in return for concessions by the Labour Party. (One such concession was the standing down of the Labour candidate in Pembrokeshire to enable Major Gwilym Lloyd George to win the seat.) Thus, Mr Wyatt contended, there was nothing in the Socialist tablets to prohibit a Lib-Lab arrangement.

What form should this arrangement take? In general, the party which had been third in the 1959 poll was to stand down—though sometimes the party with the larger vote should do so 'because it might be appropriate to the type of area'. (In fact Mr Wyatt in no case suggested that the Liberals should withdraw where in 1959 they had obtained more votes than Labour.) Mr Wyatt drew

[39] W. Wyatt, 'My Plan for a Lib-Lab Pact,' *New Statesman*, 26 January 1962.
[40] ibid.

up two lists of seats where, in his view such an arrangement might profitably be made. The first list comprised forty-six seats which in 1959 the Conservatives had won on a minority of votes cast. The Liberal would withdraw in (for example) South East Derbyshire, Rugby and North Hull; Labour in North Cornwall, Dulwich and Torrington. Mr Wyatt's second list comprised fifty-one seats which the Conservatives had won with an overall majority of under 4,000. Here the Liberal would withdraw in (for example) Pudsey, Chislehurst and Central Norfolk; Labour in Tavistock, North East Croydon and Galloway.

The Liberal reaction to proposals for a pact was chilly. Mr Edwin Malindine, the president of the party, stated firmly that there would be no deal with Labour or with any other party.[41] The prospective Liberal candidate for South Battersea was sacked for 'persistently advocating election pacts between Labour and Liberal'. While Mr Grimond wrote that 'it is very kind of Mr Wyatt to admit that we Liberals could be useful allies—just when the public opinion polls show that it is the mounting Liberal, not the Labour challenge that the Tories have to fear in Orpington—and that it is Labour which is splitting the progressive vote there'. It was, said Mr Grimond, flattering to see Labour sharpening its knives over whether to make an election alliance. But why did Mr Wyatt want one? Because he saw no other way of keeping up the 'remotest pretence' that the Labour Party was intact and holding on to the prospect of power. 'We certainly don't want an electoral pact between Liberals and the Labour Party in its present state. Liberals did not want to be tied up with the Labour machine . . . A realignment on the Left can only come about as the result of a shake-up, which will throw together those who really think alike and who want to change things in a radical direction.'[42]

X

The significance of the argument about an electoral agreement did not lie in any real chance of its coming about. What the argument

[41] At a South Oxfordshire Liberal Association dinner, reported *Daily Express*, 30 November 1961.

[42] J. Grimond, 'No Thanks, Woodrow', *Time and Tide*, 8 February 1962, p. 16.

reflected was the self-confidence of the Liberals, and the unease about the future which persisted among certain members of the Labour Party. Though Mr Wyatt's scheme would almost certainly have benefitted the Liberals, while leaving the Labour Party's gains problematical, the proportions of hostility in both parties were about equal. There seems no reason to doubt that at this time Mr Grimond genuinely thought the Liberals would eventually replace Labour as the principal opposition party. At the very least he was confident enough to believe that his party's future did not have to be mortgaged to electoral agreements. And, on the face of it, things looked bright enough. Liberal Party income had doubled to around £55,000 in the two years since the 1959 election. Headquarters staff had increased from twenty-five or so to a total of fifty. The party had over fifty salaried workers throughout its regional federations in England and Wales. Party membership had passed the 250,000 mark. True, the closing down of the *News Chronicle* was a blow, the impact of which was not softened by the belated attempt to save the paper made by the Liberal leadership. But the *Chronicle* had not perhaps contributed much to the post-1955 revival; and, in any case, there was still the *Guardian*. There was also the weekly *Time and Tide* which had been acquired by the young and rich Liberal priest, the Revd. Timothy Beaumont. Above all, the Liberal Party was being given increasing attention in the Conservative and Labour Press and on television. There could be little complaint about the amount of publicity which the party was being accorded.

Furthermore, in a curious way Liberalism had become smart. Confessions like 'Oh, I'm a Liberal,' delivered in a gay but defiant tone of voice, were to be heard at parties. And this increasing social (though not necessarily political) sophistication of the party was reflected in the choice of parliamentary candidates. Though there was nothing comparable to the pre-1959 influx of nationally-know 'personalities'—like Mr Ludovic Kennedy, Mr Robin Day and Miss Jacqueline Mackenzie, among others—there was a pronounced tendency for men and women in the more glamorous occupations to feel a sudden urge to stand as Liberal candidates. Nor was this in any way discouraged by Liberal officials. Quite the reverse. A well-known television producer was invited to become a candidate in a Twickenham pub. A journalist who had previously evinced no interest in politics was persuaded to stand at a by-election. (He came second in the poll.) Another journalist, who was covering a by-election, was asked by the local Liberal agent whether he would be interested in standing as a candidate. Though these methods were perhaps a tribute to Liberal enterprise, they were hardly calculated to produce a stable corpus of parliamentary candidates; and, in fact, the Liberals had a much larger number of withdrawals and re-adoptions than either of the other parties.

XI

But Mr Eric Lubbock, of Orpington, Kent, could by no stretch of language be described as a fly-by-night Liberal. He lived in the constituency. He was a member of the local council. And on 14 March 1962 it appeared that Mr Lubbock had started something new in British politics. Could it be that, after all, the reorganization of the Liberal Party was at last to produce a thumping political dividend? For Mr Lubbock had done the seemingly impossible. He had turned a 15,000 Conservative majority into a Liberal majority of 8,000. The result was:

E. R. Lubbock (Liberal)	22,846
P. Goldman (Conservative)	14,991
A. Jinkinson (Labour)	5,350
Liberal majority	7,855

What did it mean? Who were the people that had put Mr Lubbock into Parliament? What would happen next? A well-known psephologist deftly manipulated his slide-rule and solemnly informed the then chairman of the Conservative Party, Mr Iain Macleod, that if the Orpington performance were repeated all over the country the Conservatives would lose every single seat they held (except in Northern Ireland).

The Liberal Party executive, meeting in London, unanimously resolved that 'responding to the clearly expressed desire of the electorate as shown in recent by-elections and confirmed in public opinion polls, the Liberal Party declares its intention to place in the field at the next general election candidates sufficient in numbers and ability to provide the nation with the choice of an alternative Government. To achieve this aim the executive of the party therefore calls upon Liberals in all constituencies throughout the United Kingdom to mobilize in active support of their local associations and to ensure the speedy adoption well in advance of the general election of prospective parliamentary candidates by well-organized Liberal associations.'

It was the call to arms.

CHAPTER VII

HIGH TIDE AND AFTER

THE former Conservative M.P. for Orpington, Mr Donald Sumner, had throughout his life cherished the ambition, modest enough by any standards, of becoming a county court judge. In October 1961 his ambition was realized when he was given a judgeship on the Kent circuit. Since that time Orpington had had no M.P.: Mr Martin Redmayne, the then Conservative Chief Whip, was thought to be waiting for the new electoral register to appear. There was some impatience in the constituency, for in January 1962 two hundred electors of the Petts Wood ward petitioned the Chief Whip to move the writ as soon as Parliament reassembled. Mr Redmayne, however, took his time, and it was the middle of March before the election was held.

So much has been written about this contest, both at the time and subsequently, that to add to the volume may seem a work of supererogation. Yet in the few years since the by-election a certain Orpingtonian mythology—not, by the way, discouraged by the Liberals—has grown up, and it is as well to put matters in perspective.

The first misconception is that the result came as a most tremendous surprise to everyone concerned. And so, in a sense, it did. But though most politicians and political observers believed that, on balance, Mr Peter Goldman would win, the possibility of a Liberal success was present in many minds, it may be even in Mr Goldman's. Three weeks before polling day he was quoted as saying that 'I have certainly never thought that the Orpington by-election was going to be a walk-over . . . the Liberal challenge is a serious challenge in the sense that we have to take them seriously.' Mr Goldman proceeded to add his quota to the public stock of seriousness by talking of the Liberals 'left wing capacity for having at least two, sometimes three, separate policies for everything that arises in politics'; Mr Grimond was absolutely determined to have the best of two worlds'; and Liberal canvassers listened 'to whatever the latest grumble is, saying "we agree" and saying they will do what they can regardless of their capabilities or whether they have the capacity to handle the problems'.[1] Whether Mr Goldman's strictures were justified or not, Liberal canvassing had certainly produced results, as may be seen from the figures in the two general elections prior to 1962:

	Con.	Lab.	Lib.
1955	22,166	10,230	4,610
1959	24,303	9,543	9,096

Since 1959 the Liberals had made substantial progress in local government. In May 1961—the last occasion on which the whole local government electorate was able to vote—the Liberals came first with 11,770 votes, the Conservatives second with 10,979 and Labour third with 1,715. On the local authority the Liberals held 12 seats, the Conservatives 18 and Labour 2.[2] There was thus considerable initial evidence of Liberal strength in Orpington, quite apart from a National Opinion Poll which predicted a Liberal victory.

Again, Mr Lubbock was not the perfect paradigm of the rising young middle-classes that he was made out to be. True, he was a local man, and an engineer: but he was also a Harrovian, a Blue (even though a boxing Blue) and connected with the peerage. There seems little doubt that many Orpingtonians voted for him because they thought him 'nicer' than Mr Goldman, who, a Jew by birth but an Anglican by conversion, annoyed some of the electors by putting in a somewhat ostentatious appearance at divine service. In fact both Mr Lubbock and Mr Goldman were paradoxical candidates. Mr Goldman, one of the most politically intelligent and personally sensitive of post-war Conservatives, appeared during the election as arrogant and pompous. Mr Lubbock, despite his background, was the perfect antithesis.

In addition, there was some misunderstanding about the character of the constituency. For this misunderstanding the inventors of the phrase 'Orpington man' must take some of the blame. This concept, if such it can be called, obfuscated more than it clarified. The trouble was that Orpington man's characteristics varied according to the whim of the writer concerned. At one moment Orpington man was visualized as middle-aged, hard-up, basically a sound Tory, increasingly worried about the Government's 'softness' towards the trade unions; the next moment, Orpington man

[1] *Daily Express*, 23 February 1962. [2] *Observer*, 18 February 1962.

was pictured as young, ambitious, hard-up, basically anti-Tory, concerned about the future of his young children. There is no doubt which version the Liberals themselves preferred. As one commentator put it, 'The long-term importance of Orpington seems certain to be that it will at least enable the Liberals to make a fair claim (probably not lastingly valid but at least temporarily plausible) that they are now in politics to represent the New Estate—that struggling, emerging, 'hifi', younger middle-class with its neat front-gardens, carefully disguising the burden of the mortgage rate, the anxiety of the price of the season ticket and the moral crisis over the school fees.'[3]

But the Liberals claimed both too little and too much: too little, in the sense that Mr Lubbock's support already had a broader base than the rising young middle-class; too much, in the sense that there was no sign of a repeat performance in any other Home Counties constituency. Orpington, it should be noted, is not particularly rich in the modern housing in which newly married couples tend to live; it belongs more to the inter-war period. Its only real peculiarity is that, owing to the all-night train service which runs (or ran), people who work strange hours tend to live there, particularly people who work on the East side of London; thus Orpington has a substantial quota of journalists and butchers. According to a local Conservative chairman, Orpingtonians voted Liberal for these reasons:

1. Because I am anti-Common Market.
2. Because he (i.e. Mr Lubbock) is so handsome.
3. Because I don't like Peter Goldman.
4. No answer.
5. A small number had been Liberals for many years.

'It is definitely "U",' added this Conservative, 'to vote Liberal, comparable with the leapord in the back of the car and the paper tissue, a status symbol in this somewhat narrow society.'[4]

Though Orpington was at this time the largest and brightest star in the Liberal firmament, it was not the only one. On the day before the by-election, Blackpool North had gone to the polls and the Liberal, with 35 per cent of the vote, had come close to

[3] A. Howard, 'The Message of Orpington,' *New Statesman*, 16 March 1962.

[4] Neville H. Hinton, Chairman, Knoll North Branch Conservative Association, Letter in *Daily Telegraph*, 11 December 1962.

beating the Conservative. On the same day as Orpington voted, Middlesborough East had held its by-election, and here the Conservative was forced into third place by the Liberal. The by-elections followed fast, a Bradshaw of disaster for Mr Harold Macmillan and his Government: Stockton-on-Tees (where the Liberal polled 27 per cent of the vote), Derby North (25 per cent and Conservative in third place), Montgomery (Liberal win), Derbyshire West (33 per cent and Labour in third place), and Leicester North East (34 per cent and Conservative in third place). After Leicester a distraught Mr Macmillan dismissed a third of his Cabinet. 'Greater love hath no man,' said Mr Jeremy Thorpe, 'than he lays down his friends for his life.' It was the Liberal high tide: but, even at this time, there was one disappointment. The Liberals failed to win Middlesborough West, the seat in which they expected to poll really well. With the able Mr George Scott as candidate (a local boy, moreover), all they succeeded in doing was coming in a not very spectacular third, with Labour gaining the seat from the Conservatives.

But though Middlesborough was a disappointment to the Liberals, it was still a disaster to the Conservatives. The result had been anticipated by the gloomily percipient Mr Iain Macleod, the then chairman of the Conservative Party, who shortly after Orpington had lamented that the by-election results were 'far worse than expected . . . It is idle and foolish to pretend anything else. The worst is not over. This storm is still blowing and may even increase to gale force. It may well be we may have to batten down the hatches to sail through it.'[5]

At around the same time, Mr Grimond, with typical self-depreciation, confessed himself surprised at the progress his party had made. 'I don't conceal,' he wrote, that the size of the majority at Orpington, and indeed the degree of Liberal success at Blackpool and Middlesborough surprised me. We have got much further than I realised.'[6] This meant fresh stock-taking, said Mr Grimond. Before the general election the party must have established itself so firmly that its support would not be shaken by the attempt to polarize the electorate. To do this it must get across the main outline of its policies 'to a wider audience and in simpler terms'.[7]

[5] Speech reported in *Sunday Express*, 25 March 1962

[6] J. Grimond, 'Smugness Doesn't Pay,' *Time and Tide*, 23 March 1962.

[7] ibid.

How seriously was the risk of polarization taken? The normally cautious Dr David Butler considered that the increased Liberal vote was something more than a temporary phenomenon. After the May borough council election results he wrote that 'Orpington was not just a flash in the pan . . . When the Conservatives lose every council seat they defend in Aldershot, Finchley, Kingston and Maidenhead, sensational possibilities are opened up.'[8] Two weeks later Dr Butler doubted whether Liberal support would diminish before the general election. He pointed out that in the 1955 Parliament the Liberals did exceptionally well in two by-elections—Torrington and Rochdale—but that neither of these results was as remarkable as Orpington or Paisley. Nor, continued Dr Butler, was there anything to match the Liberal achievement in Derby North or Moss Side or Worcester or even Stockton: the Liberals found it almost impossible to drop below 20 per cent of the vote. 'Some new forces,' concluded Dr Butler, 'are plainly at work.'[9]

Whatever the nature of these forces—and this is a question to which we shall return later—there could be no doubt that the Liberal Party was now taken with a seriousness it had not evoked for many years. People actually rushed to join the party. Mr Edwin Malindine, the president, claimed that recruits were 'flooding' headquarters in London; panels were hard at it interviewing more than 150 people who, since Orpington, aspired to be parliamentary candidates.[10] Over ten people had volunteered on the day of the result itself.[11] Well-known Conservatives who joined the party at this time included Mr James Lemkin, the former chairman of the Bow Group; Sir Frank Medlicott, a National Liberal Norfolk M.P. until 1959; and Mr Howard Johnson, the idiosyncratic ex-Conservative M.P. for Brighton, Kemptown.[12] From the Left there came Mr P. Asterley Jones, the former Labour M.P. for Hitchin; Mr Henry Usborne, the former M.P. for Birmingham, Yardley; and Mr Morris Janis, a former Labour candidate, who within six weeks of joining the Marylebone Liberal Association was elected its chairman.[13]

[8] *Sunday Times*, 13 May 1962.
[9] ibid. 27 May 1962.
[10] Report in *The Times*, 7 May 1962.
[11] *Guardian*, 20 March 1962.
[12] In the case of Mr Lemkin this was a re-joining of the party.
[13] *Evening Standard*, 24 May 1962.

For a short time there was even a comic doubt about where Mr Christopher Mayhew's sympathies lay. The trouble arose from a Liberal poster which appeared in the window of his Wimbledon house at the time of the local elections. The East Woolwich Labour party protested—Mr Mayhew was M.P. for the constituency—and he took the poster down. His children, he explained, had put it in the window without his knowledge: but he admitted error: he should, he said, have taken it down straightaway. Mr Mayhew also promised that 'to avoid any further controversy I shall not vote. (No Labour candidate was available.) I admit I have made a mistake. What was meant to be simply an anti-Tory gesture was misunderstood as a serious pro-Liberal move. I blame myself. It gives a wrong impression of where I really stand.'[14]

There were, in addition to the new recruits, even more solid benefits from the by-election successes. The most welcome was probably money. In the first ten weeks of the previous year Liberal income had come in at the rate of about £1,000 a week. In the equivalent period of 1962 the rate was £1,500 a week. After Orpington the flow increased; and the party Treasurer, Colonel Ronald Gardner-Thorpe, raised the target for 1962 from £100,000 to £150,000.[15] One result of this increase in funds was that the party was able to employ more professional agents.[16]

But more important than the recruits, more important even than the money, was the effect the by-election results had on common opinion. A famous National Opinion Poll published shortly after the Orpington result disclosed the following replies in answer to the question: How would you vote if there was a general election tomorrow?:[17]

Liberal	30·0
Labour	29·9
Conservative	29·2
Others	0·9
Don't know	10·0

[14] *Daily Telegraph*, 10 May 1962.
[15] N. B. Maunsell, 'Cashing in on Orpington,' *Time and Tide*, 5 April 1962. Colonel Gardner-Thorpe had himself made money by buying up old-fashioned houses and converting them into flats and offices.
[16] See *The Times*, 1 September 1962.
[17] *Daily Mail*, 28 March 1962.

When the Don't knows were eleminated the figures were:

Liberal	33·7
Labour	33·5
Conservative	32·8

A Gallup Poll in April 1962 put Liberal support somewhat lower, at 22 per cent; in September a slightly different poll was published which is worth reproducing.[18] Gallup repeated a question last asked in February 1950: Would you be likely to vote for the Liberals if you thought they (a) would win only a few seats, (b) were likely to hold the balance, (c) would obtain a majority? The replies were:

	September 1962	February 1950
Few seats held	20 per cent	12 per cent
Balance held	37	28
Majority	41	31

The Conservative Party was alarmed. Central Office issued a five-page document arriving at a figure of £4,000 million—the equivalent of eleven shillings on the income tax—as the cost of Liberal proposals. Lord Hailsham did not quite return to his best denunciatory form of 1958, that other Liberal *annus mirabilis*, but he tried hard. 'It is quite certain,' he said, 'that if all the people who threatened to vote Liberal got into a room together and discovered each other's ideas there would be a civil war and they would have to be separated by the police.'[19] Lord Eccles adopted that condescending tone for which he is renowned. 'The Liberals,' he declared, 'are essentially suburban. They are products of the outer sections of our bigger cities. What they know about agriculture they have learned from geraniums in their window-boxes. And what they know about industry they have learned from books and pamphlets.'[20]

At this point it is as well to pause and recollect the political situation in 1962. The Conservative Party was not so much drifting as completely stationary. It was waiting for Mr Edward Heath to return from Brussels. Meanwhile the pay pause, such as it was, continued. The Labour Party had resolved its difficulties over defence, but—at least until Gaitskell's great Common Market speech

[18] *Daily Telegraph*, 19 September 1962.
[19] Quoted in *Daily Express*, 8 May 1962.
[20] Quoted in *Daily Mail*, 5 November 1962.

at the Brighton Conference—did not present a very inspiring spectacle. The movement towards the Liberal Party, in these circumstances, can be considered at two different levels. It can be seen as a basically materialistic revolt against the Conservatives; a revolt against the mortgage rate and the price of a season ticket and even the cost of school fees. (Though of course it is probable on statistical grounds alone that only a small proportion of those who actually voted Liberal had ever paid a school bill in their lives. For some reason, however, the cost of school fees always figures in newspaper commentaries on non-working class concerns.) On another level, the Liberal vote of 1962 can be seen as the expansion of a more generalized dissatisfaction with the condition of England and the attitudes thereto of the major political parties.

No doubt writers of letters to the press are untypical, and no doubt writers of letters to *The Times* are more untypical than most, but the following perhaps illustrates the latter kind of Liberal support: 'An increasing section of the electorate desire a Government composed of persons prepared to support legislation which is right, because it is right ethically, morally and socially. They are tired of socialist legislation designed to take what the other man has merely because it is socialist policy to share out, irrespective of merit. They are equally bored by Conservative legislation the object of which is to conserve wealth in the hands of those who already possess it, irrespective of the needs of others. They feel that in the Liberal Party they may have found young and dynamic persons whose sole political object is to do right for right's sake.'[21] This somewhat starry-eyed approach to Mr Grimond and his colleagues could well degenerate into a sterile opposition to all free politics; and, as we have seen, doing right for right's sake can be a perilous undertaking. Nevertheless this impression of the Liberals—the impression that they were not a genuine political party at all—did play an important part in their appeal.

According to the Gallup Poll, the former Conservatives who in 1962 were supporting the Liberals tended to be women rather than men and to be middle-class and middle-aged. The former Labour voters who were supporting the Liberals, on the other hand, tended to be men rather than women and to be middle-class and young. Compared to the other two parties the Liberals were a very representative group. 'They provide,' said Gallup, 'a much truer

[21] D. S. Thomson, letter in *The Times*, 21 May 1962.

cross-section of the community than do either the Conservatives . . . or Labour.'[22]

But the support did not hold. Any idea that the party might actually replace Labour before the next election had to be abandoned before the year 1963 was very far under away. It is difficult to say exactly where things had gone wrong—if indeed they *had* gone wrong in the sense that the Liberal leadership could by conscious effort have altered the course of events. One commentator puts the failure as early as June 1962, when Mr George Scott failed to win the Middlesbrough West by-election: but this judgement is possibly too severe.[23]

However, the signs of decline were clearly apparent in the group of by-elections held in November 1962. The most significant of these was probably Chippenham, a seat which the party expected Mr Christopher Layton to win. In the event he came second to the Conservative, polling 33 per cent of the vote. Nor were the other results up to hopeful expectations: in Dorset South, Norfolk Central, Northants South and Glasgow, Woodside, the Liberal polled respectively 21·7, 22·5, 19·3 and 21·7 per cent of the vote, and in each contest the Liberal came third. By the standards of the dark days of the early 1950's, of course, these results were respectable enough: but by the standards of mid-1962, or even of 1961, they were a trifle deflating. And they were not the only disappointing results. In March 1963 Mr Richard Wainwright failed to defeat the Labour candidate at Colne Valley. This constituency was in Liberal eyes an even better prospect than Chippenham. Had not Lady Violet herself once tried to win it? And had not the party taken the constituency so seriously that—contrary to the usual practice—it had commissioned the National Opinion Poll to carry out a pre-election survey?[24]

Altogether, the Liberal vote in by-elections averaged 17 per cent during 1963, compared to 28 per cent during 1962. Several explanations can be advanced for the decline. First, there is the explanation—which may appear tantalogous but is not really so—that the party lost support because after Orpington it failed actu-

[22] *Daily Telegraph*, 21 May 1962. For details of Dr Abrams' *Observer* survey see ch. I above.

[23] See A. Howard, 'Grimond's Pilgrim Band,' *New Statesman*, 4 September 1964.

[24] See D. E. Butler and A. King, *The British General Election of 1964* (1965), pp. 98, 207.

ally to win seats such as those listed above (and also possibly West Derbyshire). The public, after all, are not greatly interested in percentage shares of the poll, and the public are quite right. A thirty per cent vote in a three-cornered contest does not necessarily get one into the House of Commons, and it is strength in the House of Commons that counts. Second, towards the end of 1962 the Labour Party, having recovered from its disputes over unilateralism and Clause IV, was showing greater cohesiveness; and the fact that the comrades were now behaving with a modicum of civility to one another was reflected in the by-elections. Third, as the ineptitude of Mr Macmillan's Government grew weekly more apparent during 1963, so rumours of a general election increased; in the resultant atmosphere there was an inevitable tendency towards polarization.

Above all, there was Mr Harold Wilson. Now Mr Wilson's role *vis-à-vis* the Liberals in the years 1963 and 1964 deserves some examination. It was, when one comes to think of it, a role rich in paradox. To grasp the curious situation we must go back to the Labour Party as it was before and immediately after the 1959 election. The contemporary account runs roughly as follows: before 1959 Labour was a 'cloth-cap' party; after the '59 election Hugh Gaitskell made a gallant effort to 'modernise' it; he failed on Clause IV but succeeded on the bomb; it was left to Mr Wilson to complete the process with his speech on science at the 1963 Scarborough conference. This account, though widely accepted, is largely mythological. The 1959 election was fought on a revisionist programme wholly approved by Gaitskell: the popular version of the programme, *The Future Labour Offers You* (produced under the auspices of Mr Hugh Cudlipp), was Mr Crosland's *Future of Socialism* writ small. Indeed the doctrinal battle inside the Labour Party, such as it was—for all the heavy intellectual artillery was carried by the revisionist forces—was won even before Mr Crosland's book appeared in 1956. It was won in 1954-5.

Throughout the following nine years Mr Wilson, if he was anything—and his precise views were, as C. P. Scott would have said, economised—was an anti-revisionist. Certainly he was regarded as such by the faithful party workers. The party workers were of course mistaken in thinking that Mr Wilson was on the Left; but they were correct in thinking him deeply conservative.

Mr Wilson, in fact, was a figure redolent of the 1940's: naturally enough, his whole thinking was conditioned by his experiences, at an impressionable age, in the Attlee Administration. But early in 1963 he managed to free himself from his past and from his deepest beliefs. It was a triumph of presentation. Where Gaitskell had failed, Mr Wilson succeeded. He was more revisionist than the revisionists. The operation was consciously planned and brilliantly executed. 'What,' asked a political journalist of Mr Wilson, 'do you see yourself as doing?' 'I am,' he replied, 'making myself acceptable to the suburbs.'

In these circumstances, what was Mr Grimond to do? In the event he did what he had done so often before: nothing. Just as in 1959-61 there was no attempt to exploit the divisions inside the Labour Party, so in 1963-64 there was little effort to challenge Mr Wilson's claim that he best represented the new men. One need not be too hard on Mr Grimond. There was probably very little he could have done. At any rate, his declared policy was not to produce anything new but to consolidate the gains already made. Nineteen sixty three, he declared in a message to the constituency associations, would not be a time for producing great quantities of new Liberal policy. The task would be to prepare for a general election. As the election approached, said Mr Grimond, politicians and political commentators became obsessed by manœuvres for party advantage. If the Liberals were to succumb to such temptations, they would not win, or deserve to win, the support which was steadily coming their way; and 'if we needed any lesson in political honesty we have to look at the recent sorry history of the Tory party, blown this way and that by those winds of change the Tories so belatedly discovered, a party now seen to be united behind no purpose except an attempt to cling to office.'[25]

And, in a way, Mr Grimond was right about the Conservatives. For 1963 was the year not only of the Profumo affair but also of modernization as a fashionable Conservative concept; the year of Beeching and Buchanan and Robbins. Though it is legitimate enough to say that the Conservatives 'took over' various Liberal policies, there remains one misconception about the timing of the take-over. Liberal and Labour politicians subsequently claimed that modernization was a post-Macmillan phenomenon, an attempt to give Sir Alec Douglas-Home a less antique aura. In fact Mr

[25] *The Times*, 28 December 1962.

Macmillan had planned the modernization campaign before he was taken ill: evidence for this can be found in the Conservative pamphlet *Acceleration*, particularly in Mr Macmillan's introduction to it.

At about the same time the Liberals published the first draft of *Partners in a New Britain*, which embodied policy decisions, taken by recent assemblies, that had been approved by the party executive. The intention was to amend the document after the Brighton Assembly. New items of policy approved by resolution would be included, and account taken of comments made in debate on the three sections of the document. The first section, 'Reshaping Britain', was concerned with regional government, parliamentary and civil service reform, taxation, agriculture, transport and housing; the second, 'People as Partners', with industrial relations, wages, consumer protection, social security, education and the health services; and the third, 'Towards World Order', with world disarmament, the United Nations, the Common Market, Commonwealth development, the American alliance and aid to underdeveloped countries. The chairman of the assembly agenda committee explained that the sections would be 'presented or introduced', the assembly being asked to approve or reject the draft *in toto*. While amendments would not be in order, the views expressed by delegates would be fully taken into account'.[26]

A week later the party, in its information bulletin *Current Topics*, enlarged on its plans for reform of local government on a regional basis. The members of the regional councils would be directly elected, with one member for each parliamentary constituency, and would be responsible 'for those functions which need to be planned and controlled (though not necessarily administered) over an area larger than that of any individual local authority'. The councils might take over from existing authorities responsibility for education, excluding universities, for town and country planning, for fire and police services, for some roads, and for specialized health and welfare services. The main concern of these councils would be planning the services and allocating finance: detailed administration would be left to the local authorities. The suggested natural regions were Northumbria, Solway, York, Midland, West Country, Anglia, Solent, Wessex and London.

The Times newspaper fell upon this and similar pieces of modish

[26] ibid. 3 September 1963.

thinking. 'There is', went a leader, 'a fly-paper quality about Liberal policy exercises: ideas which happen to be buzzing around at the time tend to get stuck on. This makes the proposals in the present case difficult to square one with another. Restore to Parliament the power and respect it once had. Good: but that means, supposing it could be done, that Parliament would cease to be a compliant instrument of the Government or majority party and that individual members would be able once more to act in fluid combinations of interests and views in order to restrain, overthrow, or force the hand of the Government; and that, however nice a prospect, is not the surest way of achieving smooth, purposive, centralized five-year planning with all targets hit, which is another Liberal ambition—unless of course the professional planners were to carry on regardless of the politicians, an arrangement ruled out elsewhere in the statement of policy.'[27]

But the *Spectator* was not so sure. Following the appearance of *Partners in a New Britain*, it ran a leader which, after mentioning the charges against the Liberals of Poujadism and irresponsibility, adopted a remarkably friendly tone: 'In the long term . . . what should alarm the two main parties . . . are the signs that the Liberals have used the last eighteen months to produce an intelligent and sophisticated rationalization of the vague dissatisfactions . . . [The draft Liberal manifesto] vigorously goes after the genuine problems which are worrying many people today—the growing feeling of divorce between government and subject, the structure and practice of democratic administration, the problems of economic planning and decentralization, and, above all, the question of class barriers'.[28]

It was in a modernizing mood, then, that the Liberals travelled to their Brighton Assembly. On its eve Mr Basil Wigoder, the chairman of the executive, gave a confident account of the party's fortunes. Party income before the 1959 election, he said, was £24,000: this had now been trebled. The National League of Young Liberals had had 200 branches: it now had over 500, and membership had trebled. Membership of the party immediately before the 1959 election was about 150,000: it was now about 300,000. And so on.[29]

[27] ibid. 10 September 1963.
[28] *Spectator*, 6 September 1963.
[29] *The Times*, 11 September 1963.

Yet, in an odd kind of way, the modernization theme, as presented by the platform, did not quite strike the right chord on the assembly floor. Perhaps the trouble, or part of it, lay in the composition of the audience. As one observer[29a] noted, the Liberals of 1963, as displayed at The Dome, Brighton, seemed to be either very young or very old. On the one hand there were venerable figures, of both sexes; soul-mates, one would have thought, of that famous assembly chairman of days past, Sir Arthur Comyns Carr. On the other hand there were girls and youths wearing sweaters to which were affixed C.N.D. badges. Of course there were some people in between; these were mainly those middle-aged, slightly disappointed-looking figures who are perpetual attenders at all party conferences. Judging from the appearance of the assembly floor, what was lacking was any representation of the young, ambitious technicians whom the party had so frequently claimed for its own during the preceding two years.

Naturally enough, it was the younger set which made the most noise. Its greatest triumph was the prevention of a speech by Lady Violet Bonham Carter. Picture the scene: a debate was proceeding on a resolution calling for an early general election: Lady Violet was due to speak next: then a slow handclap began in the hall. The delegates said they were tired of a sterile debate merely abusing the Macmillan government; they wanted something more constructive. The platform took the point, and poor Lady Violet had to put her notes away. Imagine, an Asquith being compelled to stay silent! Times had clearly changed, though whether for the better or not is another question. Certainly Lady Violet was treated with grave discourtesy: but, apart from this, she probably had something to say that was worth hearing.

The silencing of Lady Violet was not the young Liberals' only victory. The assembly came within a whisper of calling for votes at eighteen. A demand for an unqualified party commitment to 'a target of 500,000 houses a year for five years' was rejected by only 110 votes. (This cry was raised by some East London Liberals led by the moustachioed Mr Tudor Gates. They could by no stretch of language be described as representatives of youth. However, the younger Liberals strongly supported this somewhat unrealistic demand.) Again, the pink-shirted radical clergyman, the Revd Timothy Beaumont, won loud applause when he said that the

[29a] I think it was Mr T. F. Lindsay.

Party's policy on public schools should be examined again and 'given more teeth'. Unless this was done, he declared, the Party's object of achieving a 'new Britain based on partnership' would be nullified.[30]

But the 1963 Assembly will be remembered not so much for the signs of rebellion among the Liberal young as for Mr Grimond's closing speech. 'I intend', he said, 'to march my troops towards the sound of gunfire . . . If we return with a solid block of Liberals in the House of Commons, even if we do not hold a majority, we shall be able to influence the whole thinking of the country and the attitude of whatever party may be in power.' The enemy was complacency and wrong values, and inertia in the face of incompetence and injustice. 'It is against this enemy that we march,' said Mr Grimond. 'Other nations have rebuilt their institutions under the hard discipline of war. It is for Liberals to show that Britain, proud Britain, can do this as a free people without passing through the furnace of defeat.' Whereupon the delegates rose in a mass, applauding for nearly two minutes, waving their papers, and finally breaking into 'For he's a jolly good fellow'.[31]

The Assembly was followed by some organizational changes. Mr Grimond appointed a general election committee to run the Liberal campaign and the party organization from 1 January 1964. Financial control was placed in the hands of one Treasurer, Sir Andrew Murray. His fellow joint-treasurers took up other duties: Mr Beaumont looked after party publications, and Colonel Gardner-Thorpe concentrated on his election campaign.[32] The functions of the committee were described, in perhaps over-martial terms, as follows: 'The General Election Committee under

[30] *The Times*, 14 September 1963.

[31] One does not want to detract from the excellence of Mr Grimond's speech on this occasion, but too much should not be deduced from the enthusiastic reception it evoked. As far as party conferences are concerned, the coinage of standing ovations has been much debased of late. This is true of all parties, though the Labour Party has perhaps carried the process further than the rest. A Conference speech by a Labour leader is now considered a failure unless it is followed by a standing ovation and a tuneless rendering of 'For he's a jolly good fellow'—which with 'Auld Lang Syne' is the current Labour favourite, 'The Red Flag' and 'The Internationale' being well down in the charts. This process was probably begun with Gaitskell's 'Fight and fight again' speech in 1960.

[32] *The Times*, 19 December 1963. The members of the committee were Mr Byers (Chairman), Mr Lubbock, Lord Ogmore, Mr Malindine, Lord Wimborne, Mr Wigoder, Sir Andrew Murray, Mr Beaumont, Mr Smith, Mr Rowntree and Mr Kemmis.

the generalship of Frank Byers (still only forty-nine) makes its influence felt throughout the garrison [i.e. Liberal headquarters] . . . This is the body that takes the strategic decisions. It decided, for instance, to encourage the party to fight on the widest possible front. It also plans the places that the party leaders shall include on their speaking tours.'[33]

This question of the 'widest possible front', together with the separate, though associated, question of whether the Liberals were out for power or for the balance of power, were widely discussed during 1964. It was perhaps disingenuous of some Liberals to dismiss them as pseudo-questions: though their importance may have been exaggerated, they were real enough. After all, the party's electoral performance in mid-1964 was discouraging in the extreme—misleadingly so, it turned out later. In April the Liberals failed to win a single seat on the newly created Greater London Council; nor was their performance in the other local government elections very much more heartening.

Mr Byers tried to put as brave a face on the situation as he could. The Liberals, he said, were not depressed. 'People seem to forget the tremendous strides the Liberal Party has made in the last ten years in local government. Since 1959 we can claim a net gain of 947 seats. This contrasts with the Labour Party's net gain over the same period of 11 seats, and the Tories' net loss of 523. This puts our performance in the last few weeks into perspective. In these last local government elections we claim a net loss of about 60 in the country outside London and this is only a slight decline on our 1961 position, when we won 310 seats. In 1964 we won 266 seats. These are not the figures of a party that is taking a hell of a knock.'[34]

Whether the local election results were 'a hell of a knock' or not, worse was to come. Contrary to the expectations of commentators and the advice of Central Office, Sir Alec Douglas-Home decided to hold some May by-elections rather than allow the seats to remain unfilled until the general election.[35] The results were disastrous for the Liberal Party. At Rutherglen the Liberals did not fight at all. (Nor in June did they fight either at Faversham or at Liverpool Scotland.) At Devizes, Winchester and Bury St

[33] Christopher Martin in *Liberal News*, 27 August 1964.
[34] *The Times*, 12 May 1964.
[35] The exception was Cross-bencher in the *Sunday Express*.

Edmunds, however, the Liberals fought, and came bottom of the poll in all three constituencies. The respective percentage of the vote was 10·3, 13·2 and 7·5. At Bury St Edmunds and Devizes Mr Richard Afton and the impressive Professor Michael Fogarty both lost their deposits, while at Winchester Mr John Edwards only just saved his.

Things could hardly have been worse, and even the normally sanguine *Liberal News* felt the nip of a frost in May. 'The squeeze is well and truly on . . .', wrote Mr Laurence Grinling, 'and the next few months present the Liberal Party with a tremendous challenge. It was good therefore to see Mr Grimond's fighting words last week, and to know that the party leader, at least, has no doubts about which should be done.'[36] Mr Grimond had said that an effort must be made to emphasize first, the need for a non-Socialist radical party, second, the great effect on the other parties of a substantial Liberal vote and, third, the necessity of 'keeping vital issues alive'. Mr Grinling added that not enough constituencies remembered the leader's test of whether they should fight or not. He had never used the phrase 'wide or narrow front': what he had said was that Liberals should fight when there was 'local money, organization and political know-how.'[37]

This, of course, was the hallowed formula first laid down in the 1950s by the party council.[38] It was a formula which neatly combined the principles of anarchism and authoritarianism. However, it was not taken entirely literally. Its purity was slightly spoilt by the existence of the Thorpe Committee—a three-man committee established under the chairmanship of Mr Jeremy Thorpe to assist local associations in a small number of 'special seats'. (The other members of the committte were Mr Dominic Le Foe, the party's publicity consultant, and Mr Edward Wheeler, the chief agent.) Associations were helped with publicity, premises and staff, though certain conditions had to be fulfilled first. The role of the Thorpe Committee was minimized in order to avoid protests from those constituencies not selected for special treatment.[39]

However, Thorpe Committee or no Thorpe Committee, the

[36] *Liberal News,* 21 May 1964.
[37] ibid.
[38] For details and criticism of its application see above, ch. VI.
[39] Butler and King, op. cit. p. 100.

fact remained that Mr Grimond and his colleagues had only the most limited control over the number and placing of Liberal candidates. As Mr Grimond himself put it on television, 'We don't send people down from headquarters, we don't decide—at least I don't decide, either perhaps if we're going to fight on a broad front or a narrow front. What we say is, when there are a lot of Liberals who have, as we have, a specific and definite Liberal point of view, who have the resources and the will to put up a candidate of course they must be allowed to do so. This surely is elementary.'[40]

But nevertheless reports began to appear of a disagreement in the upper ranks of the party about the number of candidates that should stand at the election. There is little doubt that in substance these reports were correct. Lord Ogmore, Mr Malindine and Mr Hope (the Chairman of the candidates' sub-committee) were all for dying gloriously; Mr Grimond, Mr Bonham Carter and Mr Byers favoured a more circumspect approach. The conflict cannot perhaps be put any higher than that. However, the *Liberal News* reported that senior members of the executive were concerned that rumours should be squashed before they had time to undermine the party's general election effort. Though the local elections and by-elections had been disappointing, 'they did not represent an accurate picture of Liberal strength or fighting spirit throughout the country. [The executive] also believe that these are important tactical reasons why any large scale withdrawal of candidates at this stage could seriously harm the party's general election effort.'[41]

After this trailer, the executive issued a statement: the party would 'contest every seat where it is possible to fight with a reasonable organization, a good candidate and adequate finance'. There were bound to be many constituencies (the statement continued) in which either Conservative or Labour candidates did exceedingly badly. The Liberal advance over past years had not been reflected in the number of seats won. It was therefore essential to reveal party strength in as large a total aggregate vote as possible. The party had for some time been making a particular effort in those seats where, in the view of the executive, the

[40] Interview with Robert McKenzie, 'Gallery', 21 May 1964, printed *Liberal News*, 28 May 1964.

[41] ibid.

chance of winning was best.[42] Liberal prospects in such seats would be improved by the knowledge that the party was fighting with determination throughout the country.

At the time the statement was issued a party spokesman said that the number of candidates was expected to be between 250 and 400.[43] At the 1963 assembly Mr Wigoder had forecast 470. In the event 365 candidates stood—ten more than Mr Byers predicted on 3 September 1964. It could not properly be described as either a broad or a narrow front; if anything victory went to the supporters of the broad front; though Mr Byers confessed that the total 'is, quite frankly, not as much as we had hoped for'. The aim, he said, had been to get between 380 and 400.[44] Still, the increase from the 1959 total was substantial.

As the discussion over the broad and narrow fronts was proceeding, there was also a dispute about the proper object of the Liberal Party at the election. To most politicians it was apparent, certainly following the Devizes by-election, that the result would be close (though this was not at first reflected by the opinion polls). Did the Liberal Party really want to hold the balance of power? And, if it did, ought the party to say so? And, again, what course precisely would the Liberals take if they did hold the balance? These questions were earnestly discussed during the summer and autumn of 1964. Mr Grimond had given one, possibly unsatisfactory answer in the previous year. 'I am often asked', he had written, 'suppose you hold the balance, what will you do?' To this I make a two-fold answer. First, I am under no illusion about the difficulties, nor the length of the road before the Liberal Party asserts itself as the main progressive force. The next election will only be a step on the way . . . Secondly, of course, the primary decision will not be for us, unless we are returned as the bigger party, which is not what the question usually envisages. The Queen will send at some stage for the leader of another party. It will be for him to decide whether he will try to form a government, and if so what policy and if necessary what terms he will offer to which of the other parties.'[45] Mr Grimond expanded his views slightly in a television interview with Dr Robert McKenzie. He made clear

[42] cf. account of the Thorpe Committee above, p. 134.
[43] *The Times*, 30 May 1964.
[44] ibid. 4 September 1964.
[45] J. Grimond, *The Liberal Challenge* (1963), p. 316.

that he would not give any support to the Labour Party if it persisted with steel nationalization; he also suggested that he would expect Labour to advocate entry into the Common Market.[46]

Mr Desmond Banks was less cautious than Mr Grimond. To Mr Banks, holding the balance was not a state of affairs about which the party ought merely to whisper: instead it should proclaim its intention of seeking this commanding position from every available platform.[47] Some Liberals, he said, were afraid of the phrase 'balance of power'. They could not expect to form a government after the election. Yet they could secure the balance of power. 'A party which refuses to go all out for the kind of power which is within its reach is no longer in politics'. Interestingly enough, Mr Banks believed that his policy required the party to fight on a broad front: as many Liberal M.P.s as possible were needed in order to make certain of a controlling position, and also a large Liberal vote would increase the authority of the 'Liberal parliamentary party in their role of the nation's trustees'.[48]

Certainly the prospect of holding the balance was taken seriously: it was discussed, though somewhat inconclusively, at a late July meeting of Liberal leaders in the House of Commons. The formula that was eventually arrived at tried to please everyone. Lord Ogmore, the president of the party, said with apparent boldness that the Liberals would be 'aiming at power', and 'as the result will be a very close thing', they would 'undoubtedly be able to influence the exercising of it.'[49] Mr Byers, for his part, explained that the Liberals aimed not at holding the balance but at 'a decisive position' that would enable Liberal M.P.s to influence any government elected. And yet, at the same time, added Mr Byers, somewhat confusingly, it was not in the least bit dangerous for a number of Liberal M.P.s to be in the position of holding the balance of power. Oh dear me no, for 'we are a united party, we are a responsible party, and it has been made abundantly clear that what the country really wants is Liberal policy'.[50]

But what of the Liberals' wider purpose—that of replacing Labour as the principal radical party? In fact, Mr Grimond's ideas

[46] The interview took place on 21 May 1964 and was printed in the *Liberal News*, 28 May 1964.

[47] Letter to *The Times*, 14 May 1964.

[48] Speech reported ibid. 2 July 1964.

[49] *Liberal News*, 3 September 1964.

[50] Speech reported in *The Times*, 15 September 1964.

were less ambitious than this simple statement of purpose might suggest. He had always been clear in his own mind that, if the Liberals were to attain this position, they would do so in collaboration with a part, possibly the major part, of the Labour Party.[51] The Liberal dilemma was that, as a radical party, it had to attack the Conservative Government; at the same time, it would have a greater chance of arriving at an arrangement—one puts it no higher—with Labour if the Conservatives were to win a fourth successive election victory. This dilemma was never satisfactorily resolved, nor could it have been. Mr Bonham Carter, however, gave a significant party political broadcast during the course of which he said that he had 'unlimited faith in the ability of the Labour Party to lose elections'. A Conservative victory, said Mr Bonham Carter, was not only 'probable'; if one accepted the available evidence, the Conservatives would 'undoubtedly win'. Such sentiments came perhaps a little late in the day.

And yet the result of the election was undeniably an interesting one for the Liberal Party. A tiny Labour majority was unenviably more fruitful in possibilities for an eventual re-grouping than a massive Conservative win would have been . . . But such speculations belong to the next chapter.

[51] For a dissenting view see letter from Warwick Deal, prospective candidate for Honiton, *Liberal News*, 2 April 1964.

CHAPTER VIII

TILTING THE BALANCE

At the beginning of September Sir Alec Douglas-Home talked to his candidates and Mr Jo Grimond roused a Liberal rally. The campaign had started. This campaign marked the general acceptance of Mr Grimond as a superb political performer, whether on television or on the platform. Of his speech at the pre-election rally, the political correspondent of *The Times* wrote that 'one could hardly believe it was the same man who rises so diffidently in the Commons . . . if he is as effective before the cameras, on the hustings and at the daily press conferences in the election campaign as he was on Saturday he could powerfully influence the hesitating voters'.[1]

And so it proved, even though the party failed to sway quite enough voters in those suburban sects in which high hopes had been reposed. The Liberals, in short, made an impact: their television broadcasts, in one of which Miss Honor Blackman had featured, were widely praised; Mr Byers conducted the daily press conferences efficiently; above all, Mr Grimond himself was here, there and everywhere. Following a somewhat dismal and discouraging eighteen months during which the party had been pre-empted by Mr Wilson, the weeks before the 1964 election saw a recovery, a recovery which was both reflected in and assisted by the opinion polls. The Conservative Party showed some concern, and Lord Blakenham, the Tory chairman, hardly distinguished himself by exhorting the electorate to vote Labour if they could not bring themselves to vote Conservative—a piece of advice which, according to Mr Byers, would have the reverse of the effect intended.

The party fought 365 constituencies, 146 more than in 1959. It won three seats in the North of Scotland and Bodmin in Cornwall. Owing to Conservative intervention (how easily one talks of candidates 'intervening', as if they had no real business to stand!), West Bolton and West Huddersfield were lost to Labour, though at

[1] *The Times*, 4 September 1964.

Huddersfield Mr Donald Wade came within 1,400 votes of winning. Orpington was safely held by Mr Eric Lubbock, but the party failed to win Colne Valley, Torrington or North Cornwall. Liberals attained second place in 54 seats, as against 27 in the previous election. Only 52 deposits were forfeited—the most satisfactory performance in this respect since 1929. Indeed in most respects this was the most satisfactory performance since 1929. In those contests which were comparable to those of 1959[2] the mean rise in the Liberal vote was 3·8 per cent. There was little regional variation, though in central London the rise was 1·5 per cent, compared to 5·9 per cent in South East England. Even in Scotland the rise was not greater than that in the country as a whole, as the excellent results in the north were balanced by some less good ones elsewhere. The general pattern to emerge was that the Liberals did best in fairly comfortable Conservative seats; they found it more difficult to make progress in marginal or Labour-held seats.[3]

Labour was elected with an overall majority of five; Lord Ogmore had spoken truer than he knew when he had declared that 'in the coming general election the Liberal Party will be aiming at power and, as the result will be a very close thing, we shall undoubtedly be able to influence the exertion of it, as we expect a considerable increase in the number of our candidates returned'.[4] After the election, Mr Grimond took up a clear attitude. In an interview in his constituency he said that he did not intend to embarrass the Government unless it introduced measures which seemed to him to be against the public interest. He ruled out harrying. He refused to believe that the Government would nationalize steel; in general 'we shall oppose anything which we think will be against the national interests and contrary to what we fought the election on. We shall, perhaps, make constructive suggestions and exert as much influence as we can'.[5]

Mr Desmond Donnelly in the *Spectator* and Mr Woodrow Wyatt in the *Birmingham Planet* went further than this. Both wanted a new political party: President Kennedy's Democratic Party was cited as a paradigm, though this model was more emo-

[2] There were 190 of them.

[3] These figures are taken from M. Steed's contribution to D. E. Butler and A. King, *The British General Election of 1964* (1965), pp. 346f. I owe other facts about the election to this work.

[4] *The Times*, 5 September 1964.

[5] ibid. 19 October 1964.

tive than useful. Mr Wyatt called for 'an electoral pact for a radical alliance' which would be certain of victory at the next election. He said that neither the Labour Party nor the Conservative Party fitted the electoral facts of Britain. He was convinced that there were 'great stirrings in people's minds'. And he uttered the warning that if the alliance was not created the Conservatives would be back again, and for longer than before.[6] Mr Grimond, however, was cautious. There had, he said, been no approval from the Labour Government. Yet there appeared to be an area in which Liberals ought to be able to find it possible to support the Government. Mr Grimond mentioned legal reforms, the social services and (if the Labour Party would tackle it) the whole question of industrial relations and restrictive practices.[7]

Inevitably the impression was created that the Liberals were 'keeping the Socialists in'. To some extent this impression was an unfair one: in the period before the Whitsun Recess there had been 170 divisions, in which the Liberal Party had voted as follows:[8]

With the Government	41
Against	95
Abstained	3
Free vote	31

Yet the impression persisted, and not entirely unjustly, for Liberals such as Lord Byers[8a] sometimes went beyond Mr Grimond's conditions for supporting the Government. Mr Grimond had taken the line that the party would give broad support to Labour, except on matters such as the nationalization of steel. Lord Byers, however, went slightly further. Liberals, he said, should think carefully before helping to force a General Election and for 'two very good reasons'. They did not want to risk a Labour Government in office with a substantial majority, which would mean 'increased socialism'. And, said Lord Byers, it would be a national disaster to return the Conservatives.[9] Again, though Mr Desmond Banks excluded electoral pacts and coalitions, he nevertheless thought that the carrying on of government demanded 'a measure of give and take' between the parties. It might

[6] Reported ibid. 22 October 1964.
[7] See ibid. 24 October and 2 November 1964.
[8] *Liberal News*, 18 June 1965.
[8a] He had been given a life peerage by Mr Wilson.
[9] Report in *The Times*, 18 February 1965.

well be, said Mr Banks, that the days of outright parliamentary majorities were numbered. In the absence of electoral reform, co-operation between the parties could take place only on the basis of their complete independence. Agreement would be tacit rather than explicit and 'it may mean the abandonment of particular measures': but it might be a national duty to attempt it.[10]

By and large, such sentiments as these were unpopular with the party activists. The National League of Young Liberals recorded their opposition to electoral pacts; and the columns of *New Outlook* and the *Liberal News* were studded with criticisms of the leadership's alleged friendliness towards Mr Wilson's administration. For instance, Mr John Parry of Richmond wrote that 'the general public is at the moment convinced that Liberals in the Commons are supporting the Labour government, as indeed they have done on a number of highly publicised issues. Now voting on issues may be all very honest and sincere, but it is not good party politics in the present situation.'[11] Mr Peter Preston, a perceptive observer of the British political scene at constituency level, also had his doubts about the effects of the Liberal attitude upon the electorate. Analysing the Liberals' disappointing performance in the by-elections which had taken place since October 1964, he noted that 'Mr Grimond and his small team were enmeshed in the toils of Westminster, proceeding carefully, thoughtfully, pragmatically, giving support to measures on their merits—an impossibly complex series of decisions to put over at the hustings.'[12] Or, as Walter Bagehot expressed it, 'We have had many recent instances how difficult it is to give what is variously termed an "independent support" and a "friendly opposition" to a government of which you approve the general tendencies, but are inclined to criticize the particular measures. The Peelites and Lord John Russell have for several years been in general in this position, and generally with a want of popular sympathy. As they agree with the government in principle, they cannot take, by way of objection, what the country considers broad points; their suggestions of detail seem petty and trivial to others—the public hardly think of such things.'[13]

[10] *The Times*, 26 February 1965.
[11] Letter in *New Outlook*, March 1965, p. 42.
[12] *New Outlook*, April 1965, pp. 1-2.
[13] W. Bagehot, 'Essay on Brougham' in *Bagehot's Historical Essays*, ed. N. St John Stevas (New York, Anchor Books, 1965), p. 137.

In May 1965 there was an apparent shift of emphasis. In a debate on the Finance Bill, the Liberals helped to bring the Government to within three votes of defeat. Mr Grimond was asked whether this indicated a change of attitude. He replied that it did not. The Liberals had made it clear in the debate on the 1964 Queen's Speech (he said) that there were certain questions on which the party would be bound to oppose the Government. The most obvious of these issues was steel nationalization. Equally, continued Mr Grimond, there were some Government policies which had featured in the Liberal election programme and whose implementation the party would welcome. Also, there was a large middle-area of decisions which had to be judged on a pragmatic basis.[14]

And yet, shortly after Mr Grimond had uttered these words, there was undoubtedly a significant change in his attitude. Speaking at Inverness, he said that the Government, having been in office over eight months, could no longer claim to be tidying up the mess left by its predecessor. It was now possible to discern what sort of Government this was. Had it, asked Mr Grimond, got its priorities right? Was it intent on incentives, modernization and a proper scheme for regional development? 'Unfortunately I fear the answer must be No . . . It had a great opportunity to rally progressive opinion. So far it has failed. And time is getting short.'[15] In the view of the *Liberal News*, the Inverness speech 'sets the seal upon the new attitude which has been developing among the Liberals in Parliament in recent weeks'. The behaviour of the Labour administration, its refusal to make any concessions to genuinely radical opinion, had convinced Mr Grimond and his colleagues that the Government deserved no assurance of Liberal support to strengthen its position. On the contrary, the Government needed 'the shock of another face-to-face encounter with the voters'.[16]

Earlier in the year—in March—the party had disposed of the *Liberal News* to Mr Douglas Brown.[17] It was no longer, therefore, an official party organ, though it continued to give its unequivocal support. On this occasion it seems the *News* overstated matters. Mr Grimond was certainly disenchanted with the Wilson admini-

[14] *The Times*, 12 May 1965.
[15] Quoted *Liberal News*, 4 June 1965. [16] ibid.
[17] The decision to do this was criticized by *New Outlook*, among others.

stration: but the Inverness speech amounted to something less than a declaration of total war. Instead Mr Grimond's position at this time can be put as follows: There was an increasing likelihood that the Liberals in Parliament would have to vote against the Government on a number of questions. So long as the Government retained its absolute majority, there was however no danger of its being brought down. (For even if the Liberals, by combining with the Conservatives, did manage to defeat the Government, the decision could be reversed, or a vote of confidence called for.) But suppose the Wilson Government lost its absolute majority? Then a different situation would arise. Though the Liberals would not have changed their basic position—that is to say, of regarding matters on their merits—nevertheless this position would in the new circumstances amount to opposition. Mr Wilson would hence have to call a general election.[18] The only method which Mr Wilson could adopt to prevent his hand being thus forced would be to arrive at an arrangement with the Liberals. Such an arrangement would have to be concerned not with electoral pacts or coalitions or even electoral reform but with long-term policy. And an arrangement would not be made after Labour's majority had been lost; the arrangement would have to be made first.

Mr Grimond said most of this in a radio broadcast he made at the end of June and in a *Guardian* interview with Mr Mark Arnold-Forster. 'We find many people in the Labour Party', said Mr Grimond in his broadcast, 'with whom we agree. But we could not make an agreement to keep it in office simply to go on in the way it has done these last nine months. As there has been no approach and as any approach must come from the Government, it is useless for me to speculate what changes Labour might be prepared to make. We have shown quite clearly the sort of policies we want. Collaboration in any form would entail a shift of emphasis. It would entail a joint programme on which both parties could agree. There is no sign of this so far.'[19]

Mr Grimond's attitude was heavily criticized inside the party. Mr Robert Glenton, the Liberal candidate and motoring corres-

[18] It may be that here Mr Grimond assumed too much. The circumstances in which the Prime Minister would be constitutionally bound to call an election would arise when the Liberals made a declaration of total opposition—something that Mr Grimond did not predicate, though a number of his party would have liked him to do so.

[19] Reprinted *Liberal News*, 2 July 1965.

pondent of the *Sunday Express*, wrote that his leader's broadcast had shown 'how uncompromisingly Liberal most of us are' and also 'how utterly incoherent and confused our leaders can make the simplest statement of fact . . . could not our spokesman resolve once and for all to remember that they are addressing a half-listening nation and not the London School of Economics?'[20] In addition to this criticism—that Mr Grimond was confusing everybody—there were two others. First, it was said that Mr Grimond was offering his favours too easily. He should demand a price: in this case electoral reform. And criticism of this kind, discreetly muted, came from as exalted a source as Mr Basil Wigoder, the Chairman of the Liberal Party Executive.[21] The second criticism was more basic, and related to the whole Grimond conception of a radical Liberal Party; or, rather, of a new radical party. For even those, such as Mr Emlyn Hooson, who were broadly in favour of a left-inclined Liberal policy tended to jib at the thought of their beloved party having to surrender its identity. It would not be right to describe the events following Mr Grimond's broadcast as a party crisis: nevertheless certain elements of crisis were present, and Mr Grimond clearly had some explaining to do.

'All this talk', Mr Grimond told the *Daily Mail*, 'is not about the situation now. I'm looking forward to the time when the Government no longer commands a majority. You can't just wait until three Labour Members are killed in a taxi and then say you need two months to consult your party.'[22] No matter what anyone said (he told the *Liberal News*) the government might soon find itself without a clear majority in the Commons. In these circumstances the decision about a general election would not rest solely with the Prime Minister; and the Liberal Party could not avoid some decisions which might affect the duration of the parliament. The decision, said Mr Grimond, could not simply be to stand aloof: the Liberals would at some time have to vote one way or the other, and their votes might either keep the government in power or put it out.[23]

These explanations did something to still the murmurings against Mr Grimond's friendliness towards the Labour administration,

[20] Letter ibid. 23 July 1965.

[21] ibid. 16 July 1965, reprint of *Guardian* article by Mr Wigoder. See also Donald Newby in *New Outlook*, August 1965, p. 32.

[22] Interview in *Daily Mail*, 5 July 1965.

[23] *Liberal News*, 2 July 1965.

though the Liberal parliamentary party continued to give some trouble. Towards the end of the session, in mid-summer, Mr Grimond's hand was forced: at an angry meeting of Liberal M.P.s the leadership agreed not to support the Government quite so solidly.

It was inevitable that the party assembly at Scarborough should arouse a particular interest. What was Mr Grimond going to say? As it happened he spelled out his attitude in some detail during the weeks immediately preceding the assembly.[24] This attitude differed in no material respect from that which he had adopted at the beginning of the summer: in the absence of any Lib-Lab arrangement he could not guarantee to support the Labour Government in the 1965-6 session of Parliament, though he hoped this would be possible: one would just have to wait and see: however, the Government might always be brought down on a snap vote in which the Liberals voted with the Conservative Opposition.[25] But though there was little new that Mr Grimond could very well say, curiosity at Scarborough was intense. Mr Grimond decided to gratify this curiosity by making a hitherto unscheduled speech on the first day of the assembly (a Wednesday) in addition to the leader's normal oration at the conclusion of the assembly. There was some dispute among Liberal leaders as to how far Mr Grimond should show his hand. If he told all, what on earth was he going to find to say on the Saturday? A well-known political correspondent was asked to give advice, and counselled that Mr Grimond should confine himself to ten minutes of cheerful talk for the troops. In the event Mr Grimond did not take this advice. He made a long and enthusiastically applauded speech in which, with exceptional skill, he managed to create the impression that the Liberal Party was sturdily independent and that at the same time it would have no objection to giving support to a Labour Government. He repeated once again his offer of an arrangement with Labour, though without much hope of acceptance.

Here we may pause and observe that this 1965 assembly was probably the high water mark of Mr Grimond's skill as a platform performer. His voice rising and falling in a manner which was almost Churchillian, he declared that he was interested in power,

[24] See in particular his article 'Why should the Liberals come to Wilson's aid?', *Sun*, 9 September 1965 and 'The Liberals and the Government', *Guardian*, 20 September 1965.

[25] I have disputed this view of the constitution in 'Towards a Minority Government', *Spectator*, 12 November 1965.

that the Liberal Party did not exist to keep any other party in office and that 'our teeth are in the real meat'.[26] Hardly anyone in the audience noticed that Mr Grimond could consistently be interested both in power and in keeping another (i.e. the Labour) party in office; indeed that the two might be conditional on each other. It was noticeable that, though he peppered his speech with passages hostile to the Conservatives, applause was louder for his anti-Labour observations. All in all the impression the 1965 Assembly created was that the delegates wanted above all to keep the Liberal Party a separate political entity. They were prepared to cheer Mr Grimond to the echo: but, like Mr Emlyn Hooson and other M.P.s they were not prepared to follow Mr Grimond in believing that the Party's real future lay in a new, radical party of the left which excluded fundamentalist socialists.

Mr Wilson's reaction to Mr Grimond's offer of an accommodation was on the surface cool. To tremendous applause at the Blackpool Conference, Mr Wilson promised that he would make no deals with anybody. But in a subsequent television interview the Prime Minister adopted a markedly more friendly tone. Of course, he said, he quite understood the Liberal's problems: he would not expect them to do anything contrary to their principles, just as they would not expect him to do anything contrary to his principles. However, if the Liberals could see their way towards supporting the Government on various measures, he would be very pleased to have their support.

And the Queen's Speech of October 1965 was written with Liberal support in mind. It predicated all manner of desirable social reforms upon which Labour and the Liberals were agreed. It proposed an Ombudsman. Above all, it omitted steel nationalization. Mr Grimond could nevertheless have carped. He could have said, as he had said previously, that the Government was doing nothing to secure 'incentives' or to solve the basic economic problems of the country. He could have shaken his head sorrowfully and regretted that at some unhappy time in the future he would have to lead his M.P.s into the lobbies against the Government. But Mr Grimond did not elect to do this. He said that as far as he could see the Liberals would be able to support the Government. He did not even utter a warning about the possibility of voting with the

[26] Not, as one has so often heard subsequently, 'the red meat'. But in either version it was an infelicitous metaphor.

Opposition on a 'Home Office' issue—the example he had given earlier in the year of the type of situation in which the Liberals might find themselves voting with the Conservatives. Everything considered, Mr Wilson seemed to have bought Liberal support at a bargain price. He had not even hinted at electoral reform.[27]

Despite the considerable interest which the Press showed in the Liberals, however, the voters—judging from by-elections and public opinion polls—grew less and less impressed during 1965. Earlier in the year Mr David Steel had won Roxburgh from the Conservatives: but Roxburgh, though a famous enough victory, was not in its effects another Torrington or another Orpington. In most by-elections the Liberal performance was disappointing; in the Erith by-election, catastrophic. A probable reason for the low Liberal polls was the widespread impression that Mr Grimond was 'keeping Labour in'. Another, less widely discussed, reason lay in the nature of the 'protest vote'. During the last twenty years, the Liberals have made the most progress when a Conservative Government has been in power. Moreover, the periods of outstanding success—roughly speaking, 1956-8 and 1961-3—have been periods of unpopularity for Conservative Governments. Conservative supporters who are dissatisfied with their government tend to vote Liberal; Labour supporters in like case tend to abstain. This conclusion is not wholly borne out by the polls' findings; nevertheless it is accepted as valid by most practising politicians. It follows that under a Labour Government the Liberal Party is deprived of one of its strengths, as those who are dissatisfied with the government's performance merely stay at home during by-elections.

[27] It was believed in some quarters that the gracious speech would say something of electoral reform. The Chief Whip, Mr Edward Short, had promised a few weeks previously that the Government would be sympathetic to proposals for changes in the electoral system. Broadly speaking, these changes could be of two kinds: the alternative vote, or the single transferable vote. Under each voting system the elector marks his ballot paper 1, 2, 3 and so on. Under the alternative vote, only one member is elected: the second preference of the candidate at the bottom of the poll are re-distributed until one of the candidates has an absolute majority. Under the single transferable vote the representation is more complicated and more proportional, and multi-member constituencies would have to be created. A Speaker's Conference was set up earlier in 1965 to consider electoral reform, among other matters.

POSTSCRIPT

THE GENERAL election of 1966 was, like that of 1964, something of a surprise, even though a minor one. The Liberals increased their representation in Parliament from ten to twelve. Two seats (Cardigan and Caithness) were lost to Labour. Three seats (West Aberdeenshire, Cheadle and North Cornwall) were won from the Conservatives. And one seat (Colne Valley) was won from Labour. The party put up fifty-four fewer candidates than in 1964, which led to the percentage Liberal vote dropping by 2·7 to 8·6. Dr Richard Rose points out that turnout was highest in seats which had been held by the Liberals, or in which the Liberals had done well in 1964. In seats where the Liberal candidate stood down the swing to Labour was slightly below average.[1] Further when a Liberal stood in a constituency not fought in 1964, the swing to Labour was above average. The implication is that on the whole the Liberals 'took votes away from' the Conservatives.

However, the results varied so much that generalization is difficult. For instance, one generalization which one heard in the immediate post-election period was that the 'Celtic fringe' was declining as a Liberal base and that the suburban areas were in the ascendant. As evidence for this, there were cited the defeats of Mr George Mackie at Caithness and Mr Roderic Bowen at Cardigan, and the victory of Dr Michael Winstanley at Cheadle—a Manchester suburb which had previously shown little inclination towards Liberalism. But the generalization is difficult to sustain. Counter-balancing the losses at Caithness and Cardigan were the wins of Mr James Davidson at West Aberdeenshire and Mr John Pardoe at North Cornwall. Moreover, Colne Valley (deservedly won by the persevering Mr Richard Wainwright) is spiritually, if not geographically, a member of the Celtic fringe. Nor, again, did the Liberals do spectacularly well in seats, such as Finchley, which had previously been considered winnable.

Yet it is possible to make some negative generalizations. First there was little sign of the Liberal Party replacing Labour. How, after all, could it? Mr Grimond had sometimes talked of 'replacing Labour as the principal party of radical opposition', or words to

[1] *The Times House of Commons 1966*, pp. 234f.

this effect. In 1966 Labour was the party not of opposition but of government. Secondly, Liberal support was diffused throughout the country: no one area could any longer be claimed as a fortress; and, as a corollary, no one area could be totally written off as a wilderness.

If we take these generalizations together with the facts of the current political situation—the chief of which is that Mr Wilson has a massive majority—we can reasonably make the following predictions:

1. The Liberal Party is not 'finished'. It may well add, though not spectacularly, to its existing twelve seats.

2. It is possible, as Mr Eldon Griffiths recently suggested, that the Conservative Party will attempt to come to some arrangement with the Liberals. (Compare the post-1945 period.)

3. The Liberal leadership and the party's ordinary members will alike reject any such overtures.

4. However, there remains a conflict of purpose between the leadership and the ordinary members, and an even greater conflict between the leadership and the party's inactive supporters, in regard to an eventual amalgamation of Liberal and Labour. The party's ordinary members, plus a sizeable proportion of the parliamentary party (about half of it), are insistent that the Liberals should maintain their separate identity as a political group.

This brings us back to our starting-point in this essay: the position of Mr Grimond. He belongs to that section of the parliamentary party which sees union with Labour as the party's final object, however remote it may appear at the moment. Mr Grimond, as he himself has said, cannot go on leading the party for ever; and there is reason to believe that his last farewell may be said sooner rather than later. There is also some reason to believe that he would like Mr Jeremy Thorpe to succeed him. Mr Thorpe, like Mr Grimond, belongs to the left of the Liberal Party. Indeed he is some way further to the left. Not all members of the parliamentary party would be pleased to see him take over, and it is likely that Mr Emlyn Hooson would be put up as the 'right wing' candidate against Mr Thorpe—the believer, as it would doubtless be expressed, in the absolute independence and integrity of the party.

In these circumstances a compromise candidate might well emerge. Nor would a compromise choice be due solely to Mr

Thorpe's inclination to the left, or Mr Hooson's inclination to the right. For neither politician is perhaps the ideal choice for leader. Mr Thorpe, despite (it may be because of) his undoubted brilliance, does not impress the House of Commons: in parliamentary terms, he lacks weight: he tends to be regarded, whether fairly or not, as the perpetual ex-President of the Oxford Union. Whereas Mr Hooson is in some quarters thought to be too mild-mannered, and too immersed in his legal practice, to make a wholly successful party leader.

If Mr Thorpe and Mr Hooson are eliminated, there is one obvious choice in Mr Eric Lubbock; especially since Mr Mark Bonham Carter has recently withdrawn from active Liberal politics. Whether Mr Lubbock would lead the Liberals into an amalgamation with Labour is an open question. He might, however, mould the party into a more effective parliamentary force. As has been argued elsewhere in this book, one of the party's major weaknesses has lain in its collective parliamentary performance, even though there has recently been some improvement in this regard. But, whatever happens in Parliament, the Liberal dilemma persists. It is unlikely to be resolved until after the next election, and perhaps not even then.

INDEX